Building Background Knowledge for Academic Subjects

Fundamental Reading

Rachel Somer

BASIC 2

DARAKWON

About the Author

Rachel Somer

BA in English Literature, York University, Toronto, Canada

Award-winning essayist, TOEIC developer, and author of educational books

Over ten years of experience as an English as a Second Language instructor

Fundamental Reading BASIC 2

Publisher Chung Kyudo
Author Rachel Somer
Editor Kim Minju, Jeong Yeonsoon, Kim Namyeon
Designers Park Narae, Black & White

First published in November 2019
By Darakwon, Inc.
Darakwon Bldg., 211, Munbal-ro, Paju-si, Gyeonggi-do 10881
Republic of Korea
Tel: 82-2-736-2031 (Ext. 250)
Fax: 82-2-732-2037

ISBN 978-89-277-0858-2 54740
978-89-277-0856-8 54740 (set)

www.darakwon.co.kr

Photo Credits
GregGrabowski (p. 30), Juan Aunion (p. 33), Jack.Q (pp. 106-107), Debby Wong (p. 111), lev radin (p. 111) / Shutterstock.com
Roland Unger (p. 115) https://commons.wikimedia.org/wiki/File:WadiSuraSwimmers.jpg
Clemens Schmillen (p. 115) https://commons.wikimedia.org/wiki/File:Bestias11.JPG

Components Student Book / Workbook
13 12 11 10 9 8 7 26 27 28 29 30

Fundamental Reading

BASIC 2

DARAKWON

How to Use This Book

This book has 8 chapters that cover different academic subjects. Each chapter is composed of 2 units based on interesting topics related to the subject.

Student Book

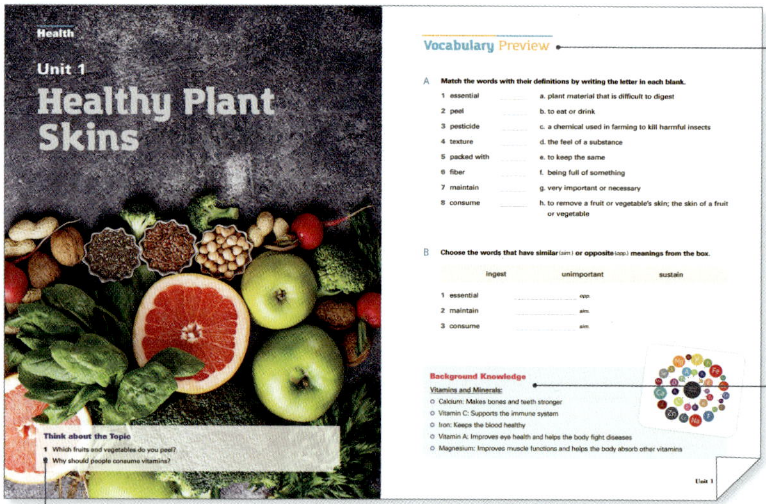
Health

Unit 1

Healthy Plant Skins

Think about the Topic

1 Which fruits and vegetables do you peel?

2 Why should people consume vitamins?

Vocabulary Preview

A Match the words with their definitions by writing the letter in each blank.

1 essential ____ a. plant material that is difficult to digest

2 peel ____ b. to eat or drink

3 pesticide ____ c. a chemical used in farming to kill harmful insects

4 texture ____ d. the feel of a substance

5 packed with ____ e. to keep the same

6 fiber ____ f. being full of something

7 maintain ____ g. very important or necessary

8 consume ____ h. to remove a fruit or vegetable's skin; the skin of a fruit or vegetable

B Choose the words that have similar (sim.) or opposite (opp.) meanings from the box.

ingest unimportant sustain

1 essential ____ opp.

2 maintain ____ sim.

3 consume ____ sim.

Background Knowledge

Vitamins and Minerals:

- Calcium: Makes bones and teeth stronger
- Vitamin C: Supports the immune system
- Iron: Keeps the blood healthy
- Vitamin A: Improves eye health and helps the body fight diseases
- Magnesium: Improves muscle functions and helps the body absorb other vitamins

Unit 1

Vocabulary Preview

Students can learn the key words from the passage and get ready to read.

Background Knowledge

Students can read brief information that will help them predict and understand the main reading passage.

Think about the Topic

Two warm-up questions are provided to motivate students to think about the topic before continuing with the unit.

QR code for listening to the passage

Main Reading Passage

The passages discuss topics that have been carefully chosen to provide academic knowledge as well as to interest students. Each passage is between 230–260 words long.

Healthy Plant Skins

Plants provide us with some of the healthiest foods on the planet. Doctors recommend that we eat five to seven servings of fruits and vegetables each day. This gives us plenty of vitamins and nutrients. Vitamins and nutrients are **essential** for good health. However, much of the vitamin content may be lost during preparation.

What is each paragraph mainly about?

1 Why fruits and vegetables are (peeled / eaten)

It's common to **peel** many fruits and vegetables. Fruits like bananas, oranges, and grapefruit have a tough outer skin. This skin is difficult to chew. It also has a poor taste. Other fruits and vegetables, such as apples and potatoes, have softer skins. Although these skins can be eaten, many people prefer not to. Some want to avoid eating **pesticides**. Others simply don't like the **texture** of the peels.

2 (Vitamins / Pesticides) and nutrients in peels

However, the peels of some plants are full of important vitamins and nutrients. For example, apple skin contains high levels of vitamin A, C, and K. It also contains high levels of calcium and potassium. Similarly, potato skins are **packed with** vitamin C and various minerals. Eating these skins can increase our vitamin and mineral intake.

Fruit and vegetable skins also contain **fiber** and antioxidants. Fiber makes people feel full for longer. As a result, we are less likely to snack in between meals. People who eat a lot of fiber have an easier time **maintaining** a healthy weight. Additionally, antioxidants may improve our health. **Consuming** antioxidants could help prevent heart disease. It could also prevent some types of cancer.

3 The benefits of fiber and ____

Antioxidant: An antioxidant is a substance that protects cells against harmful chemicals. These chemicals form when the body breaks down food or pollutants.

Words 243

What is the passage mainly about?

a. How to avoid pesticides found in foods

b. The best antioxidants to consume regularly

c. Why consuming plant skins is healthy

d. How to prepare fruits and vegetables

Unit 1

Finding the topic of each paragraph

Finding the main topic or main idea of the passage

Additional information and further learning about the topic

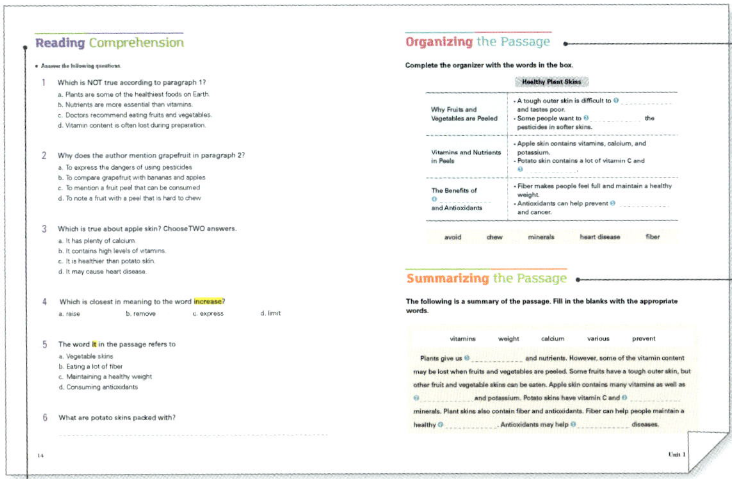

Organizing the Passage

By completing a graphic organizer, students can review and recognize important ideas and information presented in the passage.

Summarizing the Passage

Either by arranging sentences in the correct order or by completing a summary, students can review the main points of the passage once again.

Reading Comprehension

5 multiple-choice questions and 1 short-answer question are given to help students master various types of questions.

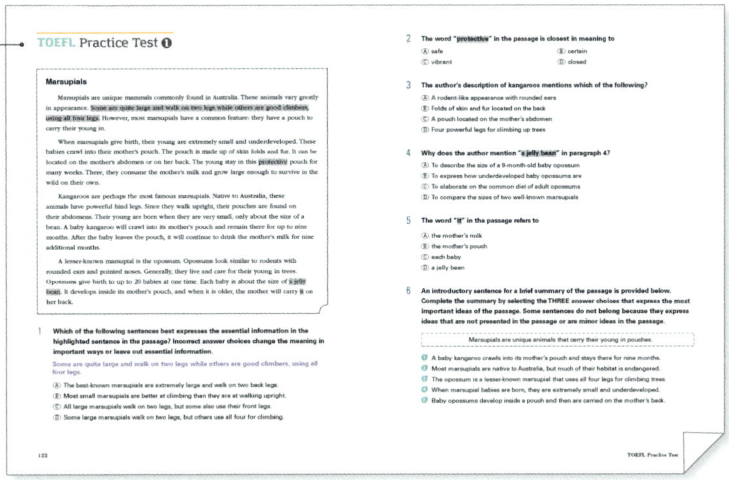

TOEFL Practice Test

At the end of the book, there is a supplementary TOEFL Practice Test section containing four passages. Each passage has six questions that frequently appear on real TOEFL tests.

Workbook

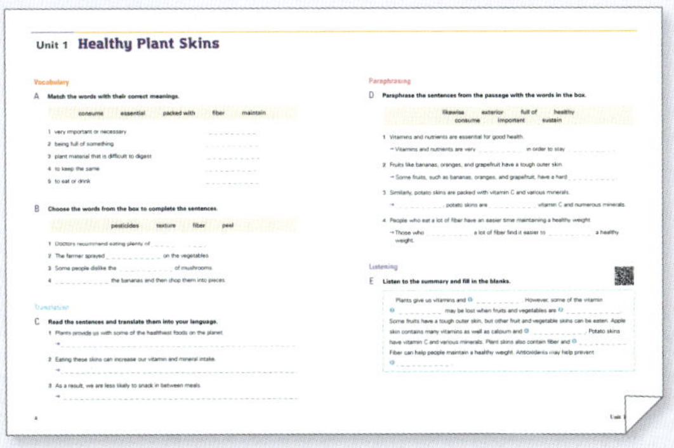

The first part contains 4 types of exercises, which provide students with a deeper understanding of the passage as well as enhanced vocabulary and language skills.

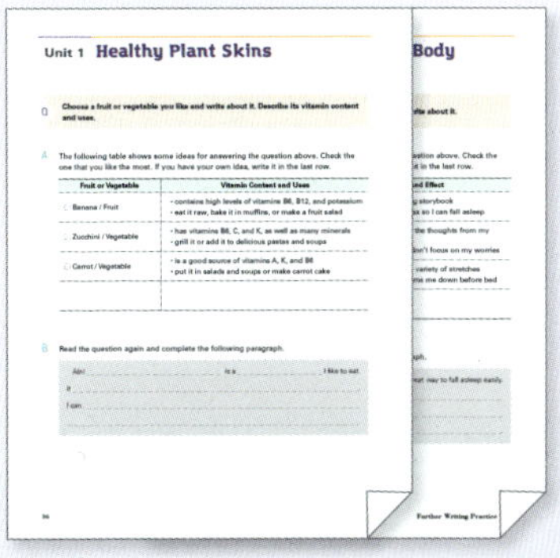

The second part presents a writing topic related to the reading passage. Students can develop their thoughts on the topic, conduct further research on their own, and learn to write a short paragraph.

Table of Contents

Chapter 1

Health

Unit 1 Healthy Plant Skins

Unit 2 Deep Sleep and the Body

Health is the state of physical and mental well-being. Scientists and doctors study processes in the mind and body in order to cure diseases. They aim to increase happiness and extend lifespans.

Health

Unit 1

Healthy Plant Skins

Think about the Topic

1 Which fruits and vegetables do you peel?

2 Why should people consume vitamins?

Vocabulary Preview

A **Match the words with their definitions by writing the letter in each blank.**

1 essential ______
2 peel ______
3 pesticide ______
4 texture ______
5 packed with ______
6 fiber ______
7 maintain ______
8 consume ______

a. plant material that is difficult to digest
b. to eat or drink
c. a chemical used in farming to kill harmful insects
d. the feel of a substance
e. to keep the same
f. being full of something
g. very important or necessary
h. to remove a fruit or vegetable's skin; the skin of a fruit or vegetable

B **Choose the words that have similar** *(sim.)* **or opposite** *(opp.)* **meanings from the box.**

ingest	unimportant	sustain

1 essential ______________ *opp.*
2 maintain ______________ *sim.*
3 consume ______________ *sim.*

Background Knowledge

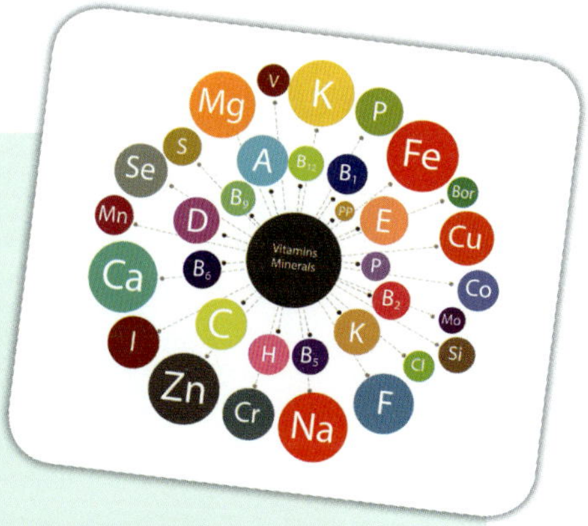

Vitamins and Minerals:

- Calcium: Makes bones and teeth stronger
- Vitamin C: Supports the immune system
- Iron: Keeps the blood healthy
- Vitamin A: Improves eye health and helps the body fight diseases
- Magnesium: Improves muscle functions and helps the body absorb other vitamins

Healthy Plant Skins

Q

What is each paragraph mainly about?

Plants provide us with some of the healthiest foods on the planet. Doctors recommend that we eat five to seven servings of fruits and vegetables each day. This gives us plenty of vitamins and nutrients. Vitamins and nutrients are **essential** for good health. However, much of the vitamin content may be lost during preparation.

P2 Why fruits and vegetables are (peeled / eaten)

It's common to **peel** many fruits and vegetables. Fruits like bananas, oranges, and grapefruit have a tough outer skin. This skin is difficult to chew. It also has a poor taste. Other fruits and vegetables, such as apples and potatoes, have softer skins. Although these skins can be eaten, many people prefer not to. Some want to avoid eating **pesticides**. Others simply don't like the **texture** of the peels.

P3 (Vitamins / Pesticides) and nutrients in peels

However, the peels of some plants are full of important vitamins and nutrients. For example, apple skin contains high levels of vitamin A, C, and K. It also contains high levels of calcium and potassium. Similarly, potato skins are **packed with** vitamin C and various minerals. Eating these skins can increase our vitamin and mineral intake.

Fruit and vegetable skins also contain **fiber** and antioxidants. Fiber makes people feel full for longer. As a result, we are less likely to snack in between meals. People who eat a lot of fiber have an easier time **maintaining** a healthy weight. Additionally, antioxidants may improve our health. **Consuming** antioxidants could help prevent heart disease. It could also prevent some types of cancer.

P4 The benefits of fiber and ________

Antioxidant: An antioxidant is a substance that protects cells against harmful chemicals. These chemicals form when the body breaks down food or pollutants.

Words 243

What is the passage mainly about?

a. How to avoid pesticides found in foods
b. The best antioxidants to consume regularly
c. Why consuming plant skins is healthy
d. How to prepare fruits and vegetables

Reading Comprehension

- **Answer the following questions.**

1 Which is NOT true according to paragraph 1?

a. Plants are some of the healthiest foods on Earth.
b. Nutrients are more essential than vitamins.
c. Doctors recommend eating fruits and vegetables.
d. Vitamin content is often lost during preparation.

2 Why does the author mention grapefruit in paragraph 2?

a. To express the dangers of using pesticides
b. To compare grapefruit with bananas and apples
c. To mention a fruit peel that can be consumed
d. To note a fruit with a peel that is hard to chew

3 Which is true about apple skin? Choose TWO answers.

a. It has plenty of calcium.
b. It contains high levels of vitamins.
c. It is healthier than potato skin.
d. It may cause heart disease.

4 Which is closest in meaning to the word increase?

a. raise　　b. remove　　c. express　　d. limit

5 The word It in the passage refers to

a. Vegetable skins
b. Eating a lot of fiber
c. Maintaining a healthy weight
d. Consuming antioxidants

6 What are potato skins packed with?

____

Organizing the Passage

Complete the organizer with the words in the box.

Healthy Plant Skins

Why Fruits and Vegetables are Peeled	• A tough outer skin is difficult to ❶ ______________ and tastes poor. • Some people want to ❷ ______________ the pesticides in softer skins.
Vitamins and Nutrients in Peels	• Apple skin contains vitamins, calcium, and potassium. • Potato skin contains a lot of vitamin C and ❸ ______________.
The Benefits of ❹ ______________ and Antioxidants	• Fiber makes people feel full and maintain a healthy weight. • Antioxidants can help prevent ❺ ______________ and cancer.

avoid chew minerals heart disease fiber

Summarizing the Passage

The following is a summary of the passage. Fill in the blanks with the appropriate words.

vitamins weight calcium various prevent

Plants give us ❶ ______________ and nutrients. However, some of the vitamin content may be lost when fruits and vegetables are peeled. Some fruits have a tough outer skin, but other fruit and vegetable skins can be eaten. Apple skin contains many vitamins as well as ❷ ______________ and potassium. Potato skins have vitamin C and ❸ ______________ minerals. Plant skins also contain fiber and antioxidants. Fiber can help people maintain a healthy ❹ ______________. Antioxidants may help ❺ ______________ diseases.

Health

Unit 2

Deep Sleep and the Body

Think about the Topic

1 How many hours do you sleep each night?

2 Why is it important to get enough sleep?

Vocabulary Preview

A **Match the words with their definitions by writing the letter in each blank.**

1 exhausted	______	a. to reach a goal
2 achieve	______	b. a series of events that repeat
3 brain wave	______	c. feeling very tired
4 cycle	______	d. muscle, organs, and skin
5 tissue	______	e. suggesting a relationship between two things
6 strengthen	______	f. to make something stronger
7 refreshed	______	g. feeling well-rested
8 linked to	______	h. electricity that moves in the brain

B **Choose the words that have similar** (*sim.*) **or opposite** (*opp.*) **meanings from the box.**

connected to	restored	fail

1 achieve ____________ *opp.*

2 refreshed ____________ *sim.*

3 linked to ____________ *sim.*

Background Knowledge

Sleep Recommendations:

- Children:
  - Babies: 14–17 hours broken up over the day/night
  - School children: 9–11 hours per night
  - Teenagers: 7–9 hours per night
- Adults:
  - Age 18–64: 7–9 hours per night
  - Age 65 and up: 7–8 hours per night

Deep Sleep and the Body

On average, most people sleep between five and nine hours a night. It's generally believed that more sleep means a healthier mind and body. However, the quality of sleep is also extremely important. People can sleep for nine hours but still feel **exhausted**. This means they did not **achieve** enough deep sleep.

Q

What is each paragraph mainly about?

P2 The stages of ________

P3 The effects of deep sleep on the (body / happiness)

There are two categories of sleep: REM and non-REM sleep. In non-REM sleep, there are three stages. During stage 1, a person begins to fall asleep. Body functions, such as heartbeat and respiration, begin to slow. In stage 2, body temperatures drop and **brain waves** slow down. Stage 3 is when deep sleep happens. It's difficult to wake from this stage, as brain waves are very slow. The brain then moves into REM sleep, which speeds up body functions again. This is when dreaming occurs.

The sleep **cycle** repeats the entire night with a full cycle lasting around 90 minutes. However, it's deep sleep that provides the most health benefits. During deep sleep, the brain repairs its cells. It also repairs damaged **tissues** and bones in the body in addition to **strengthening** the immune system. People who undergo several cycles of deep sleep will wake up feeling rested and **refreshed**.

Without enough deep sleep, people have trouble functioning. Remembering things may be difficult, which can hinder learning. Lack of deep sleep is also **linked to** certain disorders and diseases. Getting enough deep sleep could prevent *neurological disorders like Alzheimer's disease. It could also lower the risk of heart disease, stroke, and diabetes. Words 254

P4 The (dangers / benefits) of too little deep sleep

*neurological: relating to the nerves or nervous system in the human body

i **REM Sleep**: REM sleep, or rapid eye movement sleep, is a sleep stage that occurs a few times per night. Dreaming most commonly occurs during this stage.

Check the main idea of the passage.

a. Certain disorders can be cured with sleep.
b. The sleep cycle changes as people grow older.
c. REM sleep has the most benefits for the body.
d. Deep sleep is important for a healthy body and mind.

Reading Comprehension

- **Answer the following questions.**

1 Which is true about sleep according to paragraph 1?

a. The quality of sleep matters a lot.
b. Sleeping more is always beneficial.
c. Deep sleep has no real advantages.
d. Most people sleep for five hours.

2 Which is true about stage 3 of the sleep cycle?

a. Body functions speed up.
b. Brain waves are very slow.
c. The heart rate begins to slow.
d. The body starts to wake up.

3 What can you guess about the sleep cycle?

a. One 90-minute cycle occurs in stage 1.
b. Fewer sleep cycles could damage health.
c. REM sleep is when brain waves slow down.
d. Body temperatures stay the same all night.

4 The word It in the passage refers to

a. Respiration b. Deep sleep c. The brain d. Cells

5 Which is closest in meaning to risk?

a. vehicle b. situation c. system d. danger

6 What disorders could getting enough sleep prevent?

____

Organizing the Passage

Complete the organizer with the words in the box.

Deep Sleep and the Body

The Stages of Sleep	• During stage 1, a person begins to fall asleep. • In stage 2, body temperatures drop and brain ❶ ______________ slow. • Stage 3 is when ❷ ______________ sleep happens. • REM sleep speeds up body functions.
The Effects of Deep Sleep on the Body	• The brain repairs damaged tissues and ❸ ______________, and strengthens the immune system.
The Dangers of Too Little Deep Sleep	• Without enough deep sleep, ❹ ______________ may be difficult. • Lack of deep sleep is linked to certain ❺ ______________ and diseases.

waves | deep | learning | disorders | bones

Summarizing the Passage

Put the following sentences in order to make an appropriate summary. The first sentence is provided.

The quality of sleep is important for a healthy mind and body.

______ There are three stages of non-REM sleep, with deep sleep happening in stage 3.

______ Without enough deep sleep, it is harder to function, and the risk of disease increases.

______ There are two categories of sleep: REM and non-REM sleep.

______ Deep sleep provides the most benefits for the body and mind.

Chapter 2

Archaeology

Unit 3 Petra

Unit 4 Lucy

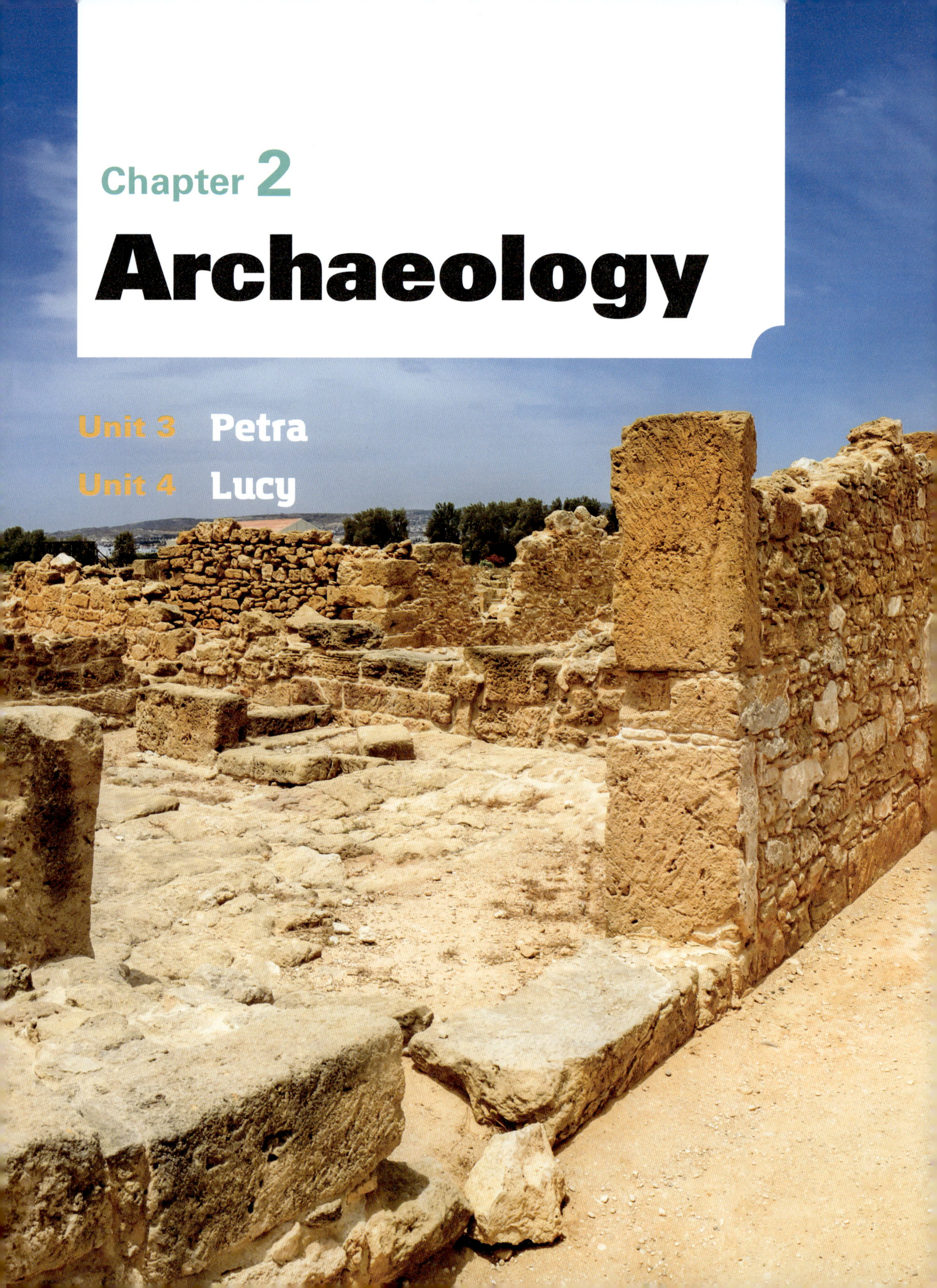

Archaeology is the study of the past through objects. Archaeologists learn about human history by studying ancient sites and remains. They also aim to understand prehistory through the study of bones and tools.

Archaeology

Unit 3

Petra

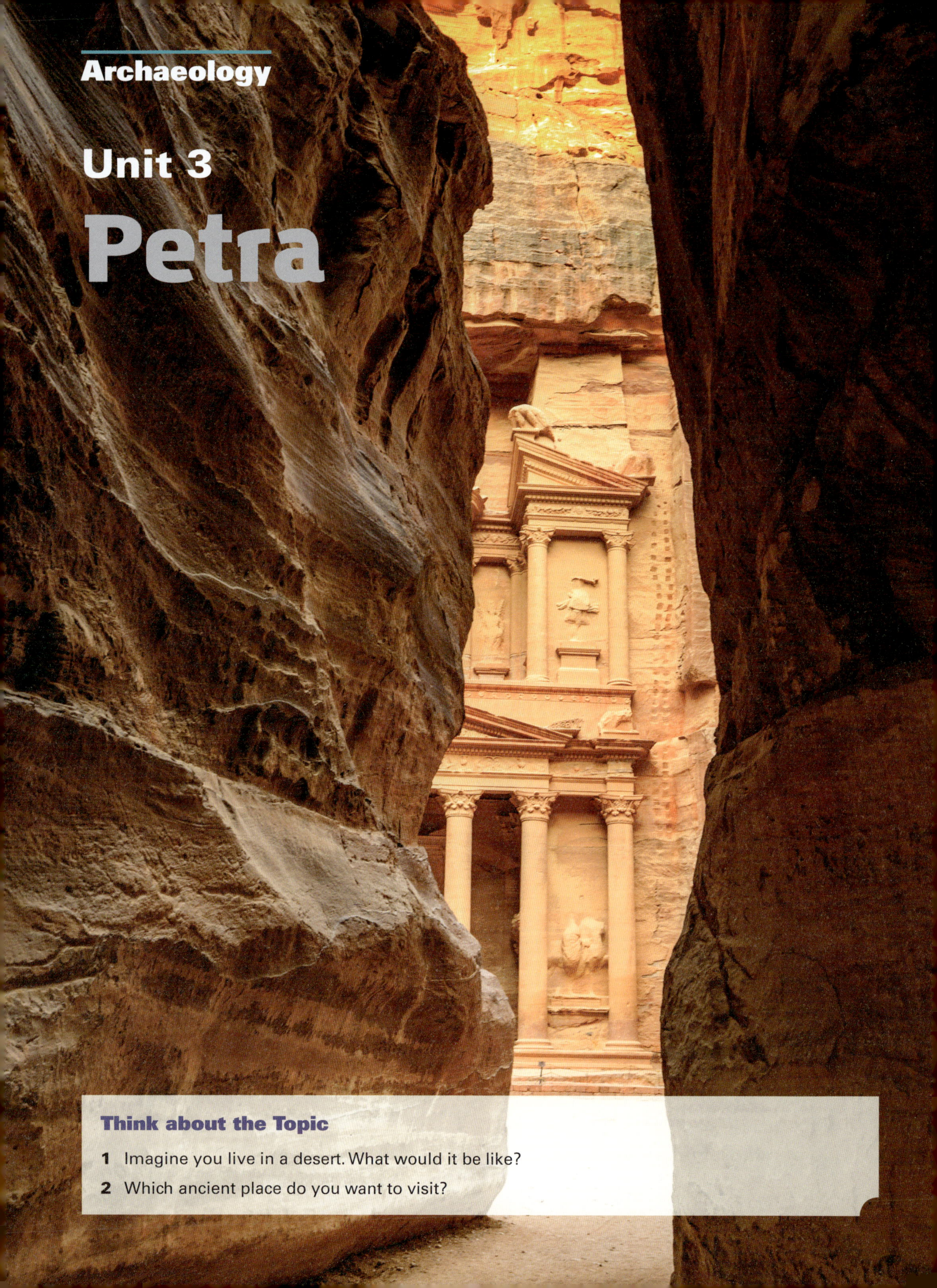

Think about the Topic

1 Imagine you live in a desert. What would it be like?

2 Which ancient place do you want to visit?

Vocabulary Preview

A **Match the words with their definitions by writing the letter in each blank.**

1 tomb	______	a. a person who goes to an unfamiliar area
2 nomadic	______	b. a place bodies are put after death
3 harsh	______	c. someone not belonging to the group
4 outsider	______	d. difficult to survive in
5 mosaic	______	e. to leave behind
6 earthquake	______	f. not living in one place for a long period of time
7 abandon	______	g. a natural event that shakes the ground
8 explorer	______	h. a pattern made from small pieces of stone or glass

B **Choose the words that have similar** (*sim.*) **or opposite** (*opp.*) **meanings from the box.**

grave	keep	gentle

1 tomb ______________ *sim.*

2 harsh ______________ *opp.*

3 abandon ______________ *opp.*

Background Knowledge

The Nabateans:

The Nabateans were an ancient Arab civilization that lived in what is now modern-day Jordan. Their capital city was called Raqmu, but is now known as Petra. They controlled this city until the Roman Empire took over their territory.

Petra

Petra is an archaeological site in modern-day Jordan. Known as the Rose City for its pinkish stone, the site is made up of caves, temples, and **tombs**. Petra is believed to be at least 2,000 years old. However, not a lot is known about the people who built it.

What is each paragraph mainly about?

P2 The (last / original) Petra

Thousands of years ago, the Nabateans lived in the deserts of Jordan. This group was originally **nomadic**. They began carving caves into stone cliffs. These caves provided shelter from the **harsh** desert. ______________, the strong cliffs made it difficult for **outsiders** to invade. Petra grew into an important trade city. Traders stopped here as they traveled through the desert.

P3 Petra after the ______________ arrived

In 63 BC, the Romans arrived in Petra. This began a new age for the city. Under Roman control, a theater that could hold 6,000 people was built. Columns were carved into rock faces. **Mosaics** were built into floors. Christianity came to Petra a few centuries later, and churches were built in the city. At its height, Petra housed 30,000 people. However, a terrible **earthquake** destroyed part of the city. After, Petra began to decline. Eventually, it was **abandoned**.

Petra was rediscovered in 1812 by a Swiss **explorer**. The city quickly became popular. Archaeologists began digging for more buildings. Today, many of the buildings are still buried under sand. Archaeologists continue to explore and learn about the city. Tourists also travel to Jordan to see the unique structures. The city has even been featured in popular films. Words 246

P4 Petra in (ancient / modern) times

Preservation of Petra: Tourism, erosion, and a lack of restoration all threaten Petra. Petra National Trust and UNESCO have been working to preserve Petra and create awareness about these dangers.

What is the passage mainly about?

a. The origins and rediscovery of Petra
b. The decline of Petra after a disaster
c. The expansion of the Roman Empire
d. The development of Nabatean culture

Reading Comprehension

- **Answer the following questions.**

1 Which is NOT true about Petra according to paragraph 1?

a. The site is made up of caves, temples, and tombs.
b. Petra got its nickname for the color of the stone.
c. Archaeologists think Petra was built in 2000 BC.
d. Petra can be found in modern-day Jordan.

2 Which is true about the Nabatean caves?

a. They contained mosaics and churches.
b. They provided shelter from the desert.
c. They housed around 6,000 people.
d. They were built by the Romans.

3 Which is the best choice for the blank?

a. For example b. Alternatively c. However d. In addition

4 Why did Petra begin to decline?

a. Traders could not find useful goods.
b. The underground rivers went dry.
c. The Roman Empire invaded the desert.
d. An earthquake destroyed part of the city.

5 Which is closest in meaning to the word featured?

a. discovered b. included c. removed d. celebrated

6 What is the condition of many of Petra's buildings today?

Organizing the Passage

Complete the organizer with the words in the box.

	Petra
The Original Petra	• The Nabateans began carving caves into stone ❶ ____________. • Petra became an important trade city in the desert.
Petra After the Romans Arrived	• A theater, columns, and ❷ ____________ were built into Petra. • Petra housed 30,000 people, but an ❸ ____________ occurred.
Petra in Modern Times	• Petra was ❹ ____________ in 1812 by an explorer. • Archaeologists and ❺ ____________ visit the city often.

tourists　　rediscovered　　cliffs　　mosaics　　earthquake

Summarizing the Passage

Put the following sentences in order to make an appropriate summary. The first sentence is provided.

Petra, also called the Rose City, is an archaeological site in modern-day Jordan.

______ Thousands of years ago, the Nabateans began carving caves into cliffs.

______ Petra was abandoned after an earthquake but was rediscovered in 1812.

______ Petra became an important place for traders to stop in the desert.

______ The Romans arrived and built mosaics, columns, and eventually churches.

Unit 4
Lucy

Think about the Topic

1 What fossils have you seen at the museum?

2 What do you think early humans looked like?

Vocabulary Preview

A **Match the words with their definitions by writing the letter in each blank.**

1 valley	______	a. the slow development of something
2 skeleton	______	b. to record in detail
3 ancestor	______	c. the remains of an ancient creature
4 upright	______	d. to divide into two or more groups
5 fossil	______	e. an early animal others have evolved from
6 evolution	______	f. a low area of land between mountains or hills
7 split	______	g. not bent; standing with one's back straight
8 map *(v.)*	______	h. a set of bones from a single creature

B **Choose the words that have similar** *(sim.)* **or opposite** *(opp.)* **meanings from the box.**

document	join	descendant

1 ancestor ______________ *opp.*

2 split ______________ *opp.*

3 map ______________ *sim.*

Background Knowledge

Australopithecus:

- Where It Lived: East Africa
- When It Lived: Between 3 and 4 millions years ago
- Height and Weight:
  - Males: around 151 cm and 42 kg
  - Females: around 105 cm and 29 kg
- Diet: Leaves, fruits, nuts, roots, seeds, insects

Lucy

What is each paragraph mainly about?

P1 Donald Johanson's (skeleton / discovery)

The year was 1974. Scientist Donald Johanson was walking through a **valley** in Ethiopia. He saw a strange bone in the ground. Johanson knew he had found something special. Over three weeks, he searched for more bones. His team dug up 47 in total. They all belonged to one amazing **skeleton**. Why was this skeleton so special?

P2 The Australopithecus (home / species)

At first, Johanson thought he had found a monkey. He quickly learned it was an early human **ancestor**. At the time, it was the oldest early human ever found. The skeleton belonged to the Australopithecus species. This species lived around 3.7 million years ago in East Africa. They were short and looked similar to apes. They were good at climbing trees. However, they could walk **upright** like humans.

P3 Why ______________ was important

Scientists nicknamed the skeleton Lucy. Only about 40% of her skeleton was found. But she is considered one of the most important **fossils**. Before Lucy was found, scientists did not fully understand human **evolution**. They believed humans and chimpanzees had a common ancestor. But they weren't sure which species came next. Lucy seemed to solve this mystery.

▲ Lucy's skeleton at the National Archaeological Museum in Madrid © Juan Aunion

P4 Theories of (evolution / chains) today

Decades later, scientists no longer believe Lucy is the key. New studies suggest that humans **split** from chimpanzees much earlier. Lucy may have been a human ancestor, but there are still many gaps in the chain of human evolution. Scientists continue to study Lucy and other fossils. They hope to one day fully **map** human evolution.

Words 238

How Lucy Got Her Name: While Lucy was being unearthed, the archaeological team listened to the song "Lucy in the Sky with Diamonds" by The Beatles. The team decided to name her after the song.

What is the passage mainly about?

a. Searching for fossils in East Africa
b. How human evolution was mapped
c. Where the Australopithecus species lived
d. The discovery and importance of Lucy

Reading Comprehension

- **Answer the following questions.**

1 The word They in the passage refers to

a. Valleys b. Weeks c. Bones d. Teams

2 Why does the author mention apes in paragraph 2?

a. To compare apes with modern humans
b. To illustrate the appearance of Lucy's species
c. To explain why Lucy could walk upright
d. To describe the features of Lucy's ancestors

3 Which is NOT true about Australopithecus?

a. It lived nearly 4 million years ago.
b. It was good at climbing trees.
c. It was an early human ancestor.
d. It split into 47 different species.

4 What does the underlined part of the passage mean?

a. Most scientists assumed chimpanzees are a human ancestor.
b. Scientists thought humans and chimpanzees came from one species.
c. Chimpanzees are no longer thought to be related to humans.
d. Apes and chimpanzees share many common ancestors.

5 Which is closest in meaning to the word gaps?

a. spaces b. requests c. parcels d. decorations

6 What do scientists hope to do one day?

Organizing the Passage

Complete the organizer with the words in the box.

Lucy	
Donald Johanson's Discovery	• In 1974, Johanson discovered a ❶ ______________ in a valley in Ethiopia.
The Australopithecus ❷ ______________	• This species lived around 3.7 million years ago. • They looked similar to ❸ ______________ but could walk upright.
Why Lucy Was Important	• Humans and chimpanzees shared a common ❹ ______________. • Lucy was thought to be the next step in evolution.
Theories of Evolution Today	• Humans and chimpanzees may have split earlier. • There are still many ❺ ______________ in the chain of evolution.

gaps ancestor apes skeleton species

Summarizing the Passage

The following is a summary of the passage. Fill in the blanks with the appropriate words.

evolution valley fossil scientists million

In 1974, Donald Johanson found a special skeleton in a ❶ ______________ in Ethiopia. This skeleton belonged to the Australopithecus species. This species lived around 3.7 ❷ ______________ years ago and looked similar to apes. Nicknamed Lucy, the skeleton is a very important ❸ ______________. Scientists believed Lucy was the key to mapping human ❹ ______________. Today, however, there are still many gaps in the chain. ❺ ______________ continue to study Lucy and other fossils. They hope to map the chain of evolution.

Chapter 3

Astronomy

Astronomy is the study of space and the objects there. Astronomers learn about planets, moons, stars, galaxies, and other bodies in space. They try to understand how these bodies originated and how they have changed over time.

Astronomy

Unit 5

The Age of the Sun

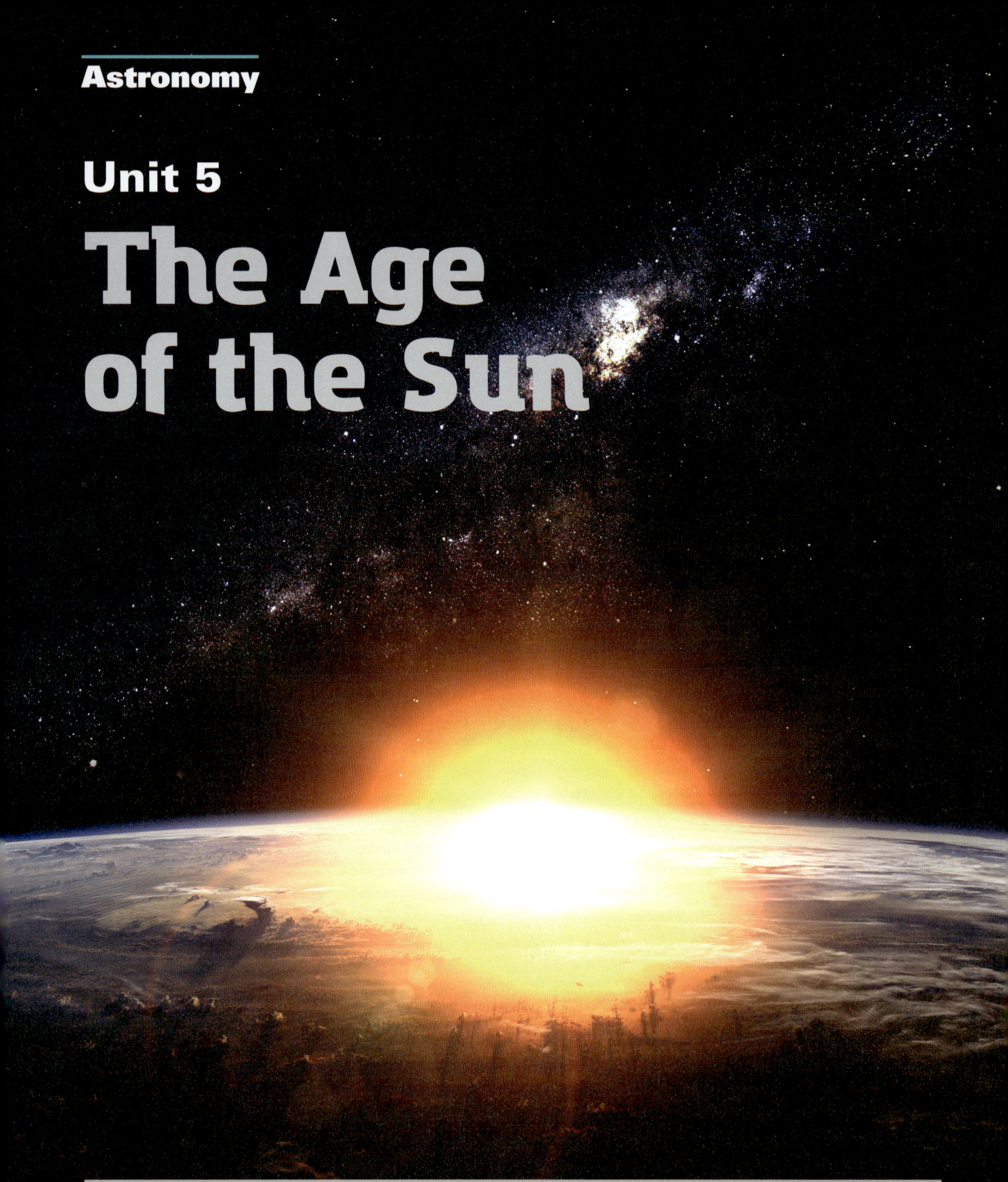

Think about the Topic

1 What have you observed through a telescope?

2 How old do you think the sun is?

Vocabulary Preview

A **Match the words with their definitions by writing the letter in each blank.**

1 transition	______	a. a change from one state to another
2 sustain	______	b. to release
3 task	______	c. to change into a gas
4 predict	______	d. a job that is done
5 expand	______	e. to grow larger
6 vaporize	______	f. having parts that are closely packed together
7 dense	______	g. to keep alive
8 expel	______	h. to make a guess about the future

B **Choose the words that have similar** (*sim.*) **or opposite** (*opp.*) **meanings from the box.**

forecast	eject	shrink

1 predict ______________ *sim.*

2 expand ______________ *opp.*

3 expel ______________ *sim.*

Background Knowledge

The Sun:

- Location: The Solar System in the Milky Way Galaxy
- Classification: Yellow Dwarf Star
- Size: 1.3 million kilometers in diameter
- Temperature: 15 million degrees Celsius at the core
- How it Works:
  - Nuclear activity sends radiation into space
  - This radiation is light and heat

The Age of the Sun

What is each paragraph mainly about?

P2 Determining the sun's ____________

P3 The (past / future) of the sun

Stars undergo many **transitions** during their life cycles. Earth's sun is currently a dwarf star. Dwarf stars are small but hot and bright enough to **sustain** life from a distance. Solar astronomers estimate that the sun is somewhere in the middle of its life cycle. This makes it approximately 4.6 billion years old.

Determining the sun's age was no easy **task**. Since the planets came together around the same time, it was useful to study the entire solar system. Solar astronomers examined the oldest objects they could find to determine the system's age. Moon rocks were particularly helpful for this. Their age gave astronomers a good idea about the sun's age, too.

Solar astronomers **predict** the sun will become a red giant in about 5 billion years. This will occur because the sun will have burned up most of its gases. Red giants are much larger than dwarf stars, which

means the sun will **expand** outward. It will become so large that it will consume the first three planets. When this happens, Earth's oceans will **vaporize**, and the planet will no longer sustain life.

The sun won't stay a red giant forever. Eventually, it will begin to die. Solar astronomers think its size will decrease until it becomes a white dwarf, a small **dense** type of star. ① The white dwarf will produce its last light and then **expel** its remaining gases. ② This will form a planetary nebula. ③ They signify the end of a star's life. ④

P4 The (death / life) of the sun

Words 253

What is the passage mainly about?

a. The age and future of the sun
b. The eventual death of the sun
c. The planets that orbit the sun
d. The size and heat of dwarf stars

i Red Giant: A red giant is a star that has begun to die. It spreads outward and becomes 100 million to 1 billion kilometers in diameter. It is cooler than a yellow dwarf star.

Reading Comprehension

- Answer the following questions.

1 What can you guess about Earth's sun?

a. It is a red giant.
b. It is small and hot.
c. It will die soon.
d. It is heating up.

2 How did solar astronomers determine the sun's age?

a. They examined the oldest objects they could find.
b. They collected rocks from numerous planets.
c. They studied the age of rocks found on Earth.
d. They guessed the ages of other nearby stars.

3 Which is NOT mentioned as an effect of the sun becoming a red giant?

a. Three planets will be consumed.
b. All of Earth's oceans will vaporize.
c. The sun will expand in size outward.
d. Earth will still be able to sustain life.

4 What is a white dwarf?

a. A small hot type of star
b. A beautiful patch of color
c. A small dense type of star
d. A large expanding star

5 Where would the following sentence best fit in paragraph 4?

Nebulae are beautiful patches of color and light.

a. 1 b. 2 c. 3 d. 4

6 What will happen to the sun after its red giant stage?

____

Organizing the Passage

Complete the organizer with the words in the box.

The Age of the Sun

Determining the Sun's Age	• Astronomers looked for the oldest objects they could find. • ❶ ______________ rocks helped them determine the sun's age.
The Future of the ❷ ______________	• The sun will become a red giant in about 5 billion years. • It will expand ❸ ______________ and consume the first three planets.
The Death of the Sun	• Eventually, the sun will become a white ❹ ______________. • Then it will expel its ❺ ______________ and become a planetary nebula.

outward	gases	moon	dwarf	sun

Summarizing the Passage

Put the following sentences in order to make an appropriate summary. The first sentence is provided.

Earth's sun is around 4.6 billion years old and is in the middle of its lifespan.

______ The white dwarf will expel its gases and become a planetary nebula.

______ The sun will later grow into a red giant and consume the first three planets.

______ Then the sun will begin to die and become a white dwarf, a dense type of star.

______ Determining the sun's age was difficult, but moon rocks helped with this.

Unit 6
Comets vs. Asteroids

Think about the Topic

1 What are comets and asteroids made of?

2 What do you think a comet looks like?

Vocabulary Preview

A **Match the words with their definitions by writing the letter in each blank.**

1 body	______	a. to combine to create something
2 orbit	______	b. not balanced in shape
3 telescope	______	c. a device used to look at planets and stars
4 form *(v.)*	______	d. what a substance is made of
5 composition	______	e. an object in space
6 vary	______	f. to differ in size or quality
7 irregular	______	g. the back end of an animal; something that looks like an animal's tail
8 tail	______	h. to move in a fixed path around an object; the rounded path an object makes

B **Choose the words that have similar** *(sim.)* **or opposite** *(opp.)* **meanings from the box.**

uneven	path	gather

1 orbit ______________ *sim.*

2 form ______________ *sim.*

3 irregular ______________ *sim.*

Background Knowledge

Celestial Bodies:

Celestial bodies are natural objects found in space. Stars, planets, and moons are all considered celestial bodies. However, much smaller objects, such as comets, asteroids, and meteors, are also categorized this way. Many objects gathered together, such as a solar system or even a galaxy, can also be called a celestial body.

Comets vs. Asteroids

Comets and asteroids are small **bodies** of matter that travel through space. Our solar system contains numerous comets and asteroids. These bodies **orbit** the sun in unique paths. Some can be seen from Earth's surface via **telescope** while others are close enough to be seen with the naked eye.

Q

What is each paragraph mainly about?

P2 Similarities and __________ of comets and asteroids

The solar system's comets and asteroids **formed** around the same time as the planets. It's believed that most comets and asteroids are about 4.5 billion years old. However, comets and asteroids have some key differences. __________, they formed in different locations. Asteroids formed quite close to the sun while comets formed much farther away. This affected their **composition**.

P3 Features of (planets / asteroids)

Asteroids are composed of metals and rock. They are not large enough to be considered planets, but they orbit the sun just like planets do. There are three types of asteroids: carbon-rich, metallic, and stony. Asteroids **vary** greatly in size. Some are quite small, but others may be several hundred kilometers wide. Because they are close to the sun, they don't contain any ice.

P4 Features of __________

Comets, on the other hand, are made up of ice, gases, and rock. They often have **irregular** orbits. Sometimes, they pass close to the sun before traveling

▸ An asteroid

▲ Comet C/2013 R1 (Lovejoy)

farther away. When a comet is far from the sun, it remains frozen. Completely frozen, it's about the size of a small town. However, when a comet passes close to the sun, some of the ice and gases melt. This creates **tails** of dust and gas that can sometimes be seen from Earth. Words 251

i **A Comet's Tails**: The sun's heat melts part of a comet. Solar radiation and winds blow this gas and dust away from the comet. This creates two separate tails.

Check the main idea of the passage.

a. Asteroids and comets have the same composition.
b. Asteroids orbit the sun in irregular patterns.
c. Comets always form far from the heat of the sun.
d. Comets and asteroids have many differences.

Reading Comprehension

- **Answer the following questions.**

1 Which is true about the solar system?

a. It is much older than most comets.
b. It is smaller than other systems.
c. It contains many comets and asteroids.
d. It has more comets than asteroids.

2 Which is the best choice for the blank?

a. Exactly b. Alternatively c. Namely d. Conversely

3 Which is closest in meaning to the word composed?

a. changed b. passed c. frozen d. made

4 Which is NOT true about asteroids?

a. They vary greatly in size.
b. They are considered planets.
c. They contain metal and rock.
d. There are three main types.

5 What does the underlined part of the passage mean?

a. The orbital path of a comet never changes.
b. Ice melts when the comet moves close to the sun.
c. Large comets spend more time far away from the sun.
d. Comets move around the sun in an uneven path.

6 How big are asteroids?

____

Organizing the Passage

Complete the organizer with the words in the box.

Comets vs. Asteroids

Similarities and Differences	• Comets and asteroids are about 4.5 billion years old. • Comets and asteroids formed in different ❶ ________________.
Features of Asteroids	• There are three types: carbon-rich, ❷ ______________, and stony. • Because they formed close to the sun, they don't have ❸ ________________.
Features of ❹ ________________	• Comets are made up of ice, gases, and rock. • When they pass close to the sun, some ice and ❺ ________________ melt.

locations comets gases ice metallic

Summarizing the Passage

The following is a summary of the passage. Fill in the blanks with the appropriate words.

orbits rock asteroids dust differences

Comets and ❶ ________________ are small bodies of matter that travel through space. Most comets and asteroids are thought to be around 4.5 billion years old. However, they have some key ❷ ________________. Asteroids are mostly made up of metals and ❸ ________________. They formed close to the sun, so they don't have any ice. Comets, on the other hand, have irregular ❹ ________________. Sometimes, they pass close to the sun before traveling farther away. When a comet passes close to the sun, some of the ice and gases melt, creating tails of ❺ ________________.

Chapter 4

Zoology

Zoology is the study of animals and other wildlife. Zoologists examine the physical characteristics of living creatures along with their behavior. They try to determine how these creatures interact with their environment.

Zoology

Unit 7

Armored Animals

Think about the Topic

1 Name an animal that has a shell. What is the purpose of the shell?

2 What are some ways animals protect themselves?

Vocabulary Preview

A **Match the words with their definitions by writing the letter in each blank.**

1 camouflage	______	a. an object used to protect against harm
2 sting	______	b. coloring that helps animals hide
3 shield	______	c. to protect against an attack
4 wound (*v.*)	______	d. the claw of a crab or lobster
5 sense (*v.*)	______	e. to pierce the skin with a stinger
6 tuck	______	f. to hurt a living creature
7 pincer	______	g. to hide an object inside something
8 defend	______	h. to feel

B **Choose the words that have similar** (*sim.*) **or opposite** (*opp.*) **meanings from the box.**

injure	attack	bite

1 sting ______________ *sim.*

2 wound ______________ *sim.*

3 defend ______________ *opp.*

Background Knowledge

Exoskeletons:

An exoskeleton is an external skeleton commonly found on insects and sea creatures. A creature with an exoskeleton usually has very soft insides. The exoskeleton protects this soft interior from harm. Creatures that have exoskeletons include crabs, cicadas, grasshoppers, shrimp, scorpions, spiders, ants, and many more.

Armored Animals

Q

What is each paragraph mainly about?

P1 How animals ______ themselves

P2 Armadillos and ______

P3 (Reptiles / Predators) with armor

Animals have many ways of protecting themselves from predators. Certain animals use **camouflage** to blend in with their surroundings. Others are more aggressive and may bite or **sting**, releasing deadly poisons. But some animals have protective armor. This armor is made up of shells or spikes. These features help keep animals safe from hungry predators.

Armadillos and porcupines are well-known armored mammals. The armadillo has bony plates that cover its back. These plates act like a **shield**. Predators have a difficult time **wounding** an armadillo. They have an even harder time eating one. Porcupines, on the other hand, are covered in sharp *quills. When they **sense** danger, they lie flat on their stomachs. Their quills stand erect, ready to pierce approaching predators.

Some reptiles also have armor. Turtles and tortoises both have hard shells that are made up of bones covered by plates. When there is danger, these animals will draw their legs and feet inside the shell. They will also **tuck** their heads inside. Predators are unable to bite through the hard shell. Turtles and tortoises remain safe while they hide inside.

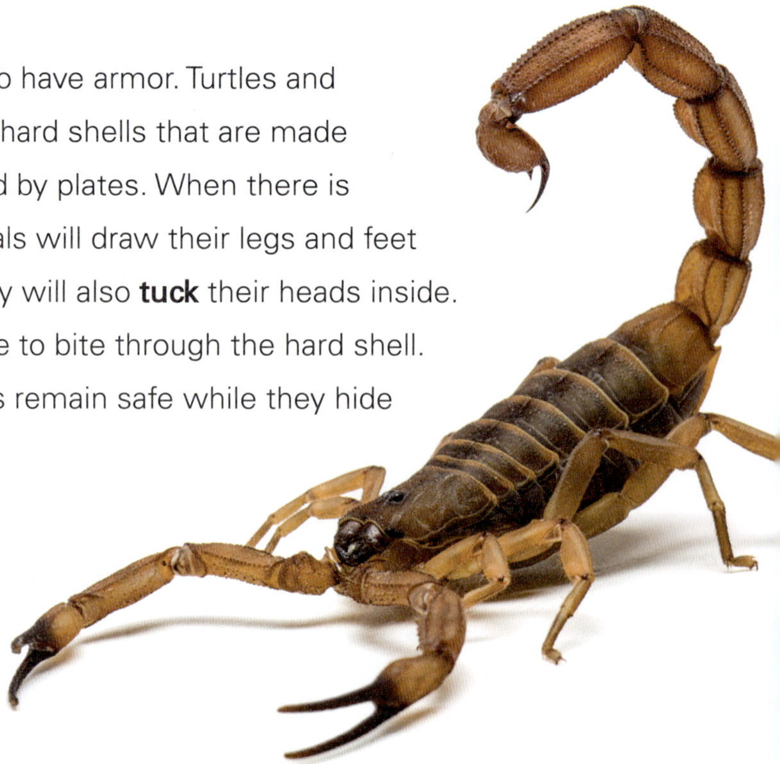

▸ A scorpion

▲ A porcupine

Armor is commonly found on many sea animals. Crabs and lobsters, for example, both have exoskeletons. ① These hard shells cover their soft insides. ② They also have **pincers** to help **defend** against predators. ③ Scorpions are land creatures, but they also have exoskeletons. ④ Words 235

P4 Animals with ____________

*quill: a sharp spike found on some animals, such as porcupines and hedgehogs

What is the passage mainly about?

a. Why animals need to have shells
b. Animals that have protective armor
c. How armor grows on sea animals
d. The strongest exoskeletons in the sea

i Exoskeletons and Growth: Some exoskeletons can increase in size. This is true for animals that can add new material to their shells, such as with snails. Other exoskeletons, however, must be shed when the animal grows too large.

Reading Comprehension

- **Answer the following questions.**

1 Why do animals have armor?

a. To survive in harsh weather
b. To locate lost family members
c. To hunt and consume larger animals
d. To stay safe from dangerous predators

2 The word They in the passage refers to

a. Porcupines b. Mammals c. Predators d. Armadillos

3 Which is true about porcupines?

a. They have a hard time eating animals.
b. They are covered in numerous plates.
c. They lie flat when predators approach.
d. They use pincers to defend themselves.

4 What can you guess about turtle and tortoise shells?

a. Predators are attracted to their shape.
b. They are primarily made up of bones.
c. It is difficult to break or pierce them.
d. They cannot grow any larger in size.

5 Where would the following sentence best fit in paragraph 4?

Like crabs and lobsters, they use their armor to defend themselves.

a. 1 b. 2 c. 3 d. 4

6 How do exoskeletons protect crabs and lobsters?

____

Organizing the Passage

Complete the organizer with the words in the box.

Armored Animals

How Animals Protect Themselves	• Certain animals use camouflage to ❶ __________ in. • Others have protective armor made of shells or ❷ __________.
Armadillos and Porcupines	• Bony plates cover an armadillo's back. • ❸ __________ are covered in sharp quills.
Reptiles with Armor	• Turtles and tortoises both have hard shells. • They ❹ __________ their legs, feet, and heads inside their shells.
Animals with Exoskeletons	• Sea creatures, like crabs and lobsters, have exoskeletons. • ❺ __________ also have exoskeletons to defend themselves.

scorpions porcupines spikes tuck blend

Summarizing the Passage

Put the following sentences in order to make an appropriate summary. The first sentence is provided.

Animals have different types of armor to protect themselves from predators.

______ All of these animals use their armor to defend themselves against danger.

______ Armadillos have bony plates while porcupines are covered in sharp quills.

______ Turtles and tortoises both have hard shells that keep them safe.

______ Certain land and sea animals have exoskeletons covering their soft insides.

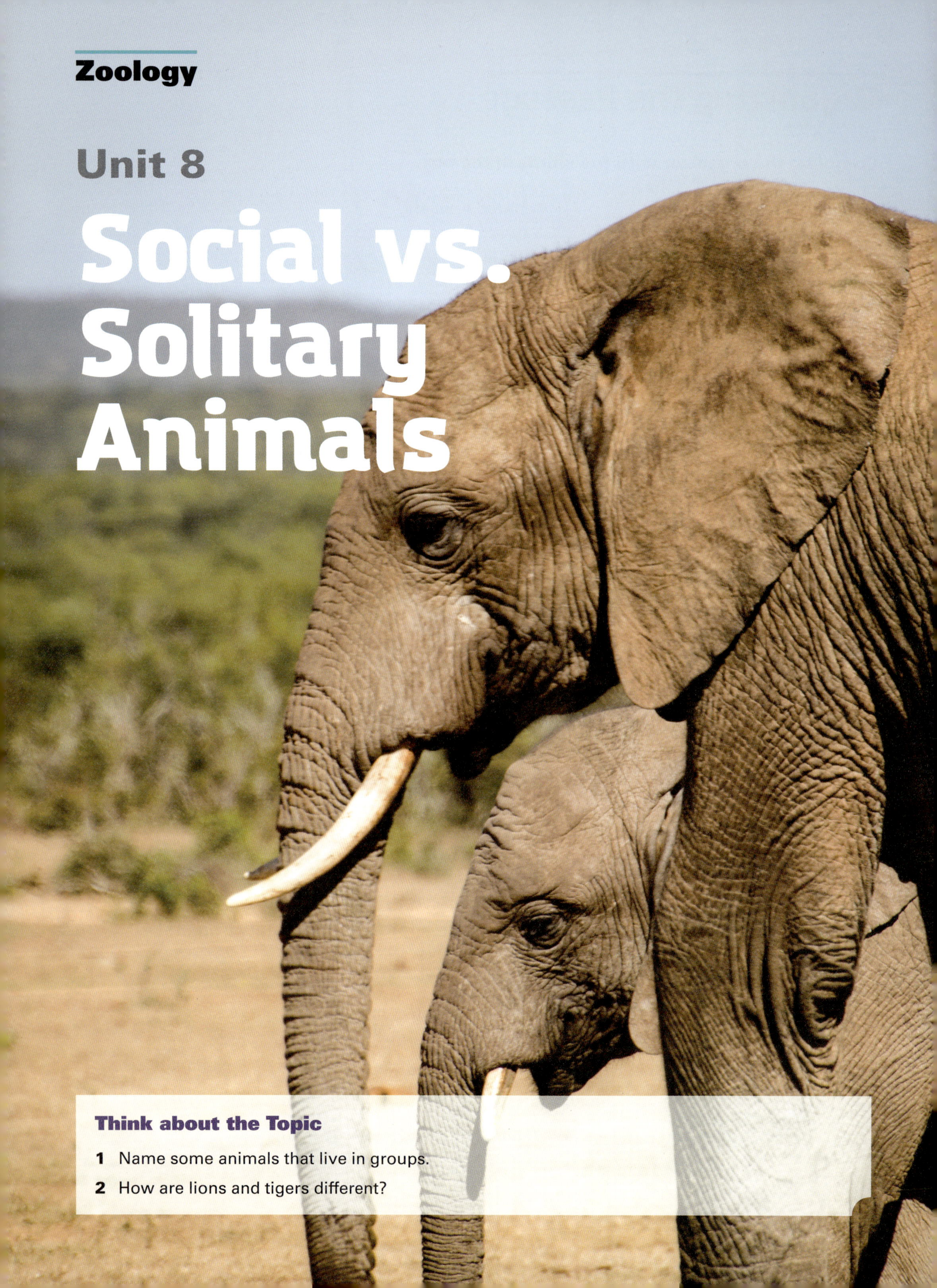

Zoology

Unit 8

Social vs. Solitary Animals

Think about the Topic

1 Name some animals that live in groups.

2 How are lions and tigers different?

Vocabulary Preview

A **Match the words with their definitions by writing the letter in each blank.**

1 savannah	______	a. because of
2 male	______	b. to follow rules or requests
3 pack	______	c. not simple
4 stalk	______	d. a group of wolves or dogs
5 obey	______	e. the babies of a particular animal
6 complex	______	f. a flat grassy area
7 offspring	______	g. a boy or a man
8 due to	______	h. to follow or chase, often secretly

B **Choose the words that have similar** (*sim.*) **or opposite** (*opp.*) **meanings from the box.**

grassland	intricate	female

1 savannah ____________ *sim.*

2 male ____________ *opp.*

3 complex ____________ *sim.*

Background Knowledge

Tiger Territories:

Tigers claim a space or patch of land as their own by marking their scent on the surrounding trees. This scent warns other tigers not to intrude. Generally, males claim a much larger territory than females, but all tigers will defend their territory. If a tiger enters another tiger's territory, a fight may break out.

Social vs. Solitary Animals

Q
What is each paragraph mainly about?

P1 Lion (females / prides)

When we think of animals living in groups, we often imagine a pride of lions roaming the African **savannah**. Typically, there is one **male** lion in the pride. There might also be three to five females and numerous cubs. A lion pride works together to hunt, defend their territory, and care for their young. Alone, they may have trouble surviving in the wild.

P2 Wolf ________

Many other species also live in groups. Wolves, for example, live in **packs** similar to lions. When they hunt, they work together to **stalk** and kill large animals. Like lions, they have a *social hierarchy. However, there are usually multiple males in the group. One male and one female are considered the leaders of the pack. The other wolves **obey** this pair.

P3 ________ herds

Non-predatory animals, such as elephants, can also live in groups. Living in a large herd keeps elephants safe from predators. However, elephants are also social animals. They form **complex** relationships with each other. An elephant herd is usually made up of one family unit. The oldest female leads her daughters and their **offspring**. A herd can be quite small, or it could include up to 50 elephants.

P4 Solitary (lions / tigers)

Some animals prefer to live alone. Tigers are extremely *territorial and do not like to share living space. Zoologists believe this is **due to** the fact that they do

not like to share food. Like all solitary animals, though, tigers aren't always alone. Rather, they must look for mates during mating season. However, once mating season is over, they return to their solitary lives. Words 256

Solitary-But-Social Animals: Some animals are both social and solitary. Usually, these animals hunt for food separately but share the same home. Orangutans, for example, are solitary-but-social animals.

*social hierarchy: a system in which people or animals are ranked above each other based on importance

*territorial: describes an animal that defends the area it lives in against outsiders

Check the main idea of the passage.

a. Lions and wolves maintain similar social hierarchies.
b. The smartest animals prefer to live in large groups.
c. All animals must live in groups at certain times
d. Some animals live in groups and others remain alone.

Reading Comprehension

- **Answer the following questions.**

1 Which is true about lion prides?

a. A pride follows one female leader.
b. There is usually one male in a pride.
c. There can be up to 50 cubs in a pride.
d. They share land with other prides.

2 Which is closest in meaning to the word **multiple**?

a. several　　b. extensive　　c. unlucky　　d. limited

3 Why does the author mention wolf pack leaders in paragraph 2?

a. To illustrate a rare way of socializing
b. To explain how wolves hunt in groups
c. To describe a pack's social hierarchy
d. To compare them to male lions

4 Who leads a herd of elephants?

a. One family unit
b. A male and a female
c. A group of offspring
d. The oldest female

5 The word **they** in the passage refers to

a. animals　　b. tigers　　c. zoologists　　d. living spaces

6 What do tigers do after mating season?

____

Organizing the Passage

Complete the organizer with the words in the box.

Social vs. Solitary Animals

Lion Prides	• A lion ❶ ________ works together to hunt, defend their territory, and care for their young.
Wolf Packs	• Wolf packs work together to ❷ ________. • One male and one female are the leaders of the pack.
Elephant ❸ ________	• Living in a large herd keeps elephants safe from predators. • An elephant herd is usually made up of one ❹ ________ unit.
Solitary Tigers	• Tigers are territorial and do not like to share space. • During mating ❺ ________, they must look for mates.

hunt   herds   season   family   pride

Summarizing the Passage

The following is a summary of the passage. Fill in the blanks with the appropriate words.

territorial   lions   female   social   non-predatory

When we think of animals living in groups, we often imagine a pride of ❶ ________. However, many other animals also live in groups. Wolves live in packs that have a ❷ ________ hierarchy. One male and one ❸ ________ are considered the leaders of the pack. ❹ ________ animals, like elephants, also live in groups. An elephant herd follows the oldest female. On the other hand, some animals prefer to live alone. Tigers are extremely ❺ ________ and do not like to share space.

Chapter 5

History

History is the study of past events. Historians examine historical evidence, such as documents, artifacts, and architecture. They aim to tell the story of the past by determining the causes and effects of events.

Unit 9

Famous Pirates

Think about the Topic

1 Where have you seen or read about pirates?

2 What are pirates famous for?

Vocabulary Preview

A **Match the words with their definitions by writing the letter in each blank.**

1 portrayal	______	a. to assume control of
2 brutal	______	b. a description of someone or something
3 capture	______	c. to catch
4 merchant	______	d. wealth in the form of money or jewels
5 fierce	______	e. harsh or violent
6 execution	______	f. when the state puts a criminal to death
7 take over	______	g. intense or aggressive
8 riches	______	h. a person or company that arranges trade or supplies goods

B **Choose the words that have similar** (*sim.*) **or opposite** (*opp.*) **meanings from the box.**

surrender	seller	gentle

1 brutal ______________ *opp.*

2 merchant ______________ *sim.*

3 take over ______________ *opp.*

Background Knowledge

The Execution Dock:

For 500 years, those caught and convicted of piracy were hung on the execution dock. This dock was visible to passing ships. Since the bodies were often left hanging for three days, they served as a reminder not to break the law. The last execution happened in 1830.

Famous Pirates

Pirates are popular TV and film characters. Production companies like Disney have made millions of dollars for their **portrayals** of pirates. But where did they get their inspiration? Writers and filmmakers often look to the past. Many fictional pirate characters are based on real pirates.

Q

What is each paragraph mainly about?

P2 The most (brutal / successful) pirate

Edward Teach is perhaps the most famous of all pirates. Better known by his nickname, Blackbeard, he was born in England in 1680. He wasn't the most successful pirate, but he is remembered as being one of the most **brutal**. During his career, he commanded four ships and around 300 men. He **captured** many **merchant** ships and often killed his prisoners.

P3 The most famous pirate ____________

Anne Bonny and "Calico" Jack Rackham are the most famous pirate couple. Bonny joined Rackham's crew while dressing and behaving like a man. A romantic relationship quickly developed between the two. Together, they were a **fierce** pirate team. However, Bonny was eventually captured along with Rackham's crew. She avoided **execution** by claiming she was pregnant. No one knows what happened to her after this.

▲ Anne Bonny and "Calico" Jack Rackham

The most successful female pirate was Ching Shih. Born in China in 1785, Ching Shih married a pirate. Upon his death, she **took over** his business. 1 Ching Shih commanded over 1,500 ships and 80,000

▲ *Capture of the Pirate Blackbeard, 1718* by Jean Leon Gerome Ferris (1920)

men. ❷ Ching Shih became so powerful that the Chinese government offered her a peace deal. ❸ She was able to keep her **riches** and retire. ❹ Words 238

P4 The most successful ________ pirate

What is the passage mainly about?

a. The most frightening pirate
b. The lives of historical pirates
c. Fictional pirate characters in film
d. How pirates were often executed

i Pirate Image: Fictional pirates are often given a similar image. This may include eyepatches, peg legs, and pet parrots. This image has been used to market books, films, and even tourist attractions.

Reading Comprehension

- **Answer the following questions.**

1 Which is true according to paragraph 1?

a. Disney saw its first success with a pirate series.
b. Writers visit real pirates when researching.
c. Historical pirates often made millions of dollars.
d. Fictional pirates are based on historical pirates.

2 Which is NOT true about Edward Teach?

a. He is thought to have been the most brutal pirate.
b. He commanded four ships and around 300 men.
c. He is better known by his nickname, Blackbeard.
d. He escaped execution and went into hiding.

3 Which is closest in meaning to the word behaving?

a. surviving b. exclaiming c. acting d. smelling

4 What does the underlined part of the passage mean?

a. There are no records of what happened to Anne Bonny.
b. Anne Bonny likely escaped to another country and retired.
c. Jack Rackham rescued Anne Bonny and the rest of his crew.
d. Anne Bonny was probably never captured or executed.

5 Where would the following sentence best fit in the passage?

This is more than all the well-known pirates combined.

a. 1 b. 2 c. 3 d. 4

6 What did Ching Shih do when her husband died?

___

Organizing the Passage

Complete the organizer with the words in the box.

Famous Pirates

The Most ❶ __________ Pirate	• Blackbeard is remembered as being the most brutal pirate. • He captured ❷ __________ ships and often killed his prisoners.
The Most Famous Pirate Couple	• Anne Bonny and Jack Rackham were a fierce pirate ❸ __________. • Bonny was captured but avoided ❹ __________.
The Most Successful ❺ __________ Pirate	• Ching Shih commanded over 1,500 ships and 80,000 men. • The Chinese government offered her a peace deal.

team　　female　　execution　　merchant　　brutal

Summarizing the Passage

The following is a summary of the passage. Fill in the blanks with the appropriate words.

captured　　commanded　　pirate　　characters　　couple

Pirates are popular TV and film ❶ __________, but many are based on real pirates. Edward Teach, better known as Blackbeard, wasn't the most successful ❷ __________. However, he was one of the most brutal. Anne Bonny and "Calico" Jack Rackham were the most famous pirate ❸ __________. Together, they were a fierce team, but Bonny was eventually ❹ __________. No one knows what happened to her. The most successful female pirate was Ching Shih. She ❺ __________ over 1,500 ships and 80,000 men. This is more than all the well-known pirates combined.

History

Unit 10

Spartan Society

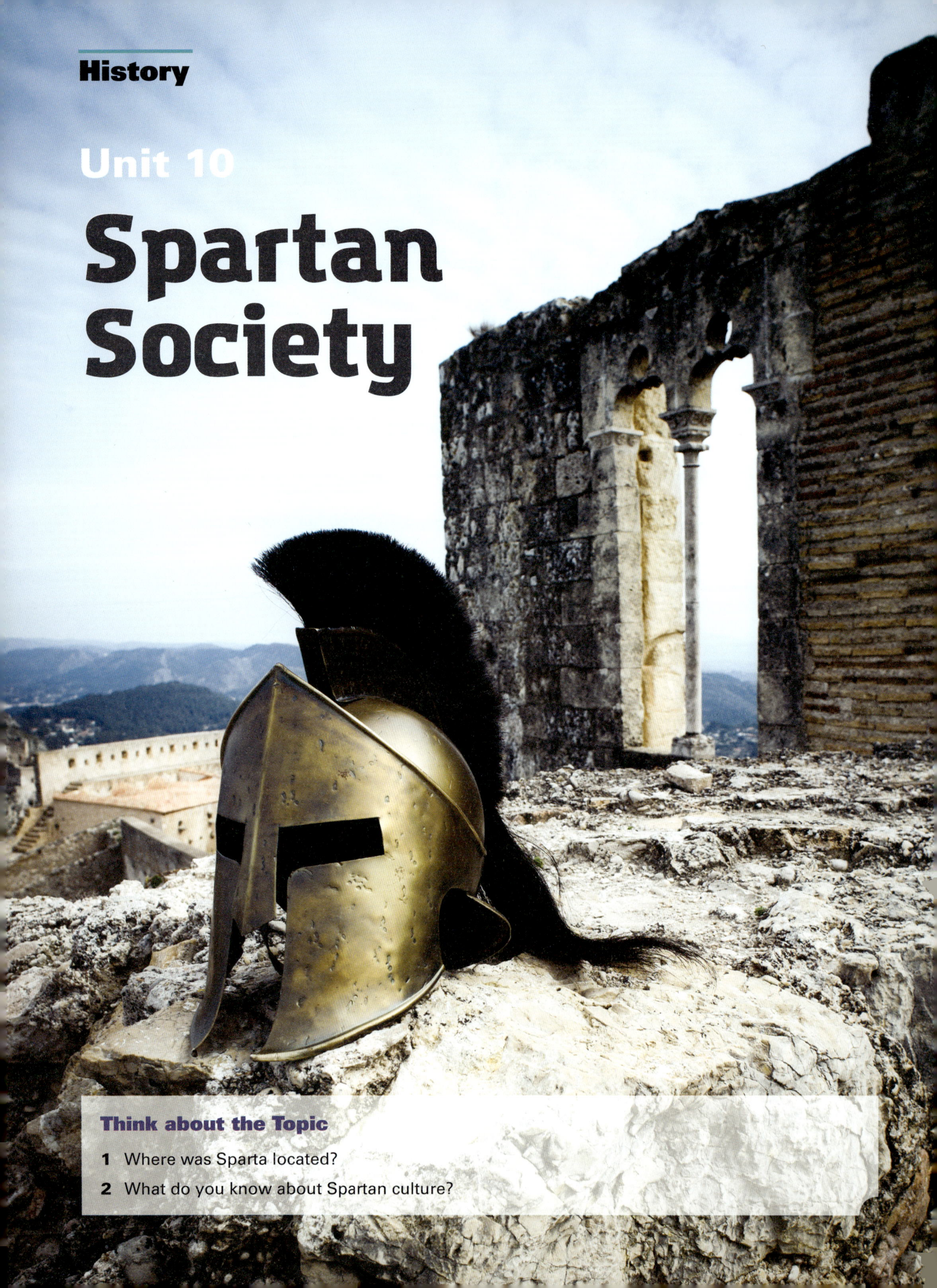

Think about the Topic

1 Where was Sparta located?

2 What do you know about Spartan culture?

Vocabulary Preview

A **Match the words with their definitions by writing the letter in each blank.**

1 warrior	______	a. a soldier or fighter
2 rigid	______	b. a person who starts an organization or town
3 generation	______	c. a group of people born within a few years
4 founder	______	d. a person forced to work without pay or freedom
5 position of power	______	e. to enter another region, often violently
6 conduct	______	f. to complete
7 invade	______	g. a ruling position, such as a king or president
8 slave	______	h. strict, not flexible

B **Choose the words that have similar** (*sim.*) **or opposite** (*opp.*) **meanings from the box.**

firm	conquer	creator

1 rigid ______________ *sim.*

2 founder ______________ *sim.*

3 invade ______________ *sim.*

Background Knowledge

Sparta:

- Location: South-eastern Greece, on the Eurotas River
- Time Period:
  - Rose to power in 650 BC
  - Conquered by the Roman Empire in 146 BC
- Government:
  - Two kings had equal power
  - Councils of elders watched over the kings

Spartan Society

Ancient Greece was made up of many cultures. Most of these cultures were very different from each other. Sparta, for example, was a **warrior** society. Spartans valued loyalty and military service more than anything. Ancient Sparta had a very **rigid** class structure. There were three main social classes: the Spartiate, the perioeci, and the helots.

Q
What is each paragraph mainly about?

P2 The Spartiate ____________

P3 The ____________ class

The Spartiate class was made up of native Spartans. These were families who had lived in Sparta for many **generations**. Usually, they could trace their ancestry back to the **founders** of the city. The Spartiate ran and served in the military. They also ran the government. They made all important decisions for Sparta. As a result, the Spartiate were wealthy and had many rights.

The perioeci were a step below the Spartiate class. These people were often *immigrants. They were not allowed to have **positions of power**. However, they had many rights and freedoms. For example, they could own land. They could also serve in the military. Usually, they **conducted** trade with other cities. This made them valuable to the Spartiate class.

At the bottom of Sparta's society were the helots. The helots were hated by most other Spartans. They originally came from a place south of Sparta called Helos. As Sparta grew, it expanded its territory. Eventually, Sparta **invaded** Helos. ① Spartans killed many helots and took others as **slaves**. ② Helots could win their freedom by serving in the military. ③ However, once they were free, they were still treated poorly. ④

P4 The (helots / Spartans)

Words 252

*immigrant: a person who comes to live in a foreign country permanently

i **Life for Spartan Children**: Children in Sparta began school at the age of seven. Boys were given intense military training. Girls were not trained for the army, but they were expected to stay fit in order to produce healthy sons when they grew up.

Check the main idea of the passage.

a. Spartans were separated into three classes.
b. The helots were the lowest Spartan class.
c. The perioeci had more rights than the helots.
d. Sparta invaded many nearby territories.

Reading Comprehension

• **Answer the following questions.**

1 What did Spartans value above all else?

a. Arts, science, and culture
b. Loyalty and military service
c. Trade and immigration
d. Invading nearby cities

2 Which is NOT true about the Spartiate?

a. They were wealthy and had many rights.
b. They immigrated from a city south of Sparta.
c. They ran and served in the Spartan military.
d. They made all important decisions for Sparta.

3 The word **They** in the passage refers to

a. The helots   b. Native Spartans   c. The perioeci   d. The Spartiate class

4 Why were the perioeci considered valuable to the Spartiate class?

a. They ran and served in the military.
b. They conducted trade with other cities.
c. They were immigrants from Greek cities.
d. They invaded Helos and took many slaves.

5 Where would the following sentence best fit in the passage?

They were often killed by other Spartans.

a. 1   b. 2   c. 3   d. 4

6 Where did the helots originally come from?

____

Organizing the Passage

Complete the organizer with the words in the box.

Spartan Society

The Spartiate Class	• They could trace their ❶ ______________ back to the city's founders. • They ran the military and the ❷ ______________ and made all important decisions.
The Perioeci Class	• They were not allowed to have ❸ ______________ of power. • They conducted ❹ ______________ and could serve in the military.
The Helots	• They were captured as slaves when Sparta invaded Helos. • They could win their ❺ ______________ but were still treated poorly.

government   trade   freedom   positions   ancestry

Summarizing the Passage

Put the following sentences in order to make an appropriate summary. The first sentence is provided.

Ancient Sparta had a very rigid class structure with three main classes.

_______ At the bottom were the helots, who were hated by most Spartans.

_______ The Spartiate were wealthy and made all important decisions for Sparta.

_______ The perioeci were a step below the Spartiate but had many rights.

_______ Helots could win their freedom, but they were still treated poorly.

Chapter 6

Meteorology

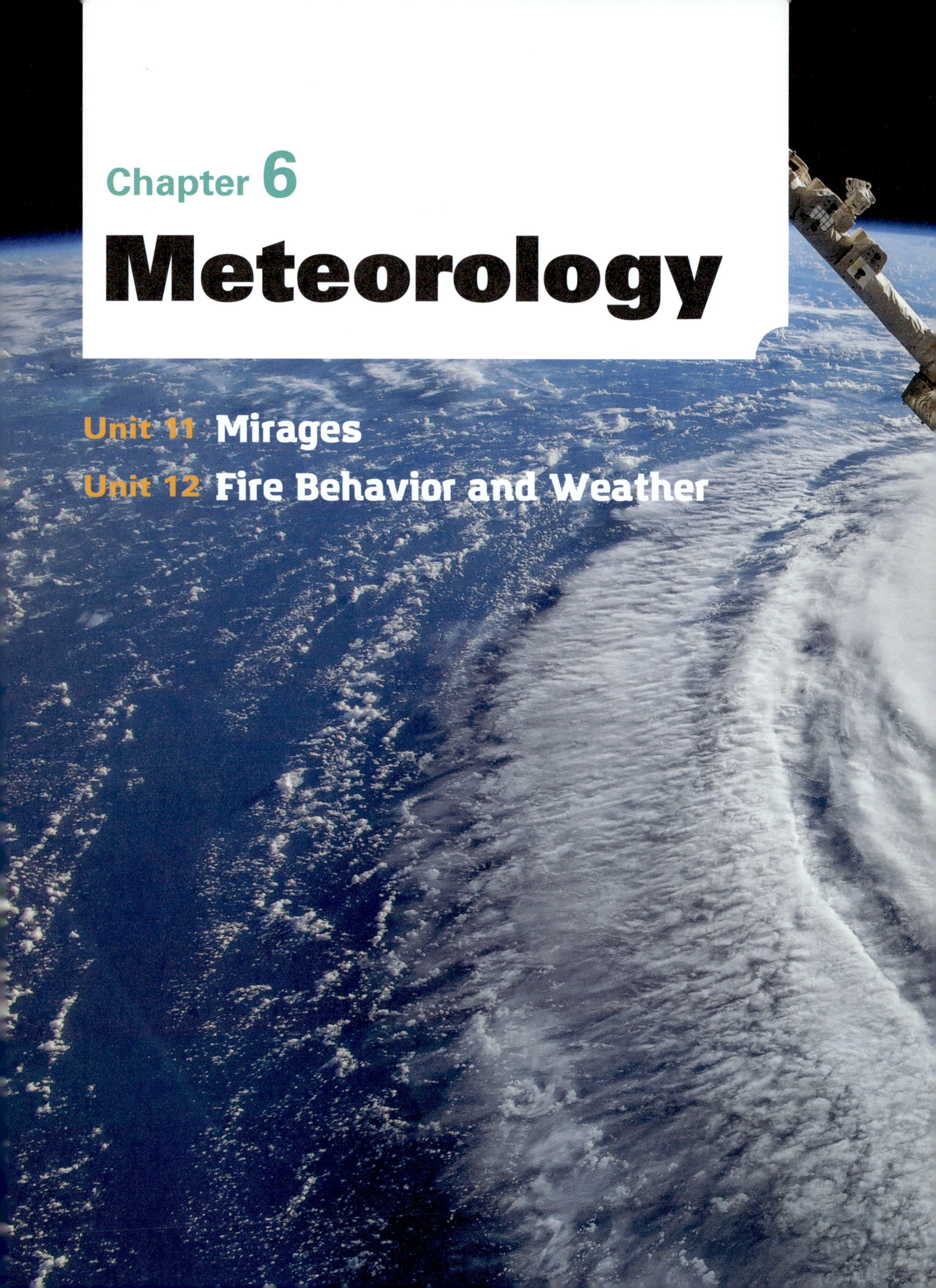

Unit 11 Mirages

Unit 12 Fire Behavior and Weather

Meteorology is the study of the planet's atmosphere. Meteorologists focus on weather processes and patterns in order to make predictions about the weather. They warn people of dangerous conditions and disasters.

Meteorology

Unit 11

Mirages

Think about the Topic

1. Have you ever seen a mirage? What did it look like?
2. Where do mirages commonly occur?

Vocabulary Preview

A **Match the words with their definitions by writing the letter in each blank.**

1 glitter	______	a. the top layer of something
2 disappear	______	b. to not be visible anymore
3 illusion	______	c. the level of heat
4 temperature	______	d. beautiful in a dramatic way
5 bend	______	e. to shine or sparkle
6 register	______	f. a curve; to shape something into a curve
7 surface	______	g. a thing that confuses the senses
8 spectacular	______	h. to notice

B **Choose the words that have similar** (*sim.*) **or opposite** (*opp.*) **meanings from the box.**

appear	amazing	straighten

1 disappear ______________ *opp.*

2 bend ______________ *opp.*

3 spectacular ______________ *sim.*

Background Knowledge

Types of Mirages:

- Inferior Mirages:
  - Appear below an object's true location
  - Occur when the ground is hotter than the air
- Superior Mirages:
  - Appear above an object's true location
  - Occur when the ground is colder than the air

Mirages

What is each paragraph mainly about?

P1 Experiencing a ____________

P2 How mirages (occur / disappear)

P3 What the human ____________ registers

Imagine you're lost in the desert. You've been walking for hours and have grown tired beneath the sun's relentless heat. Suddenly, you spot a **glittering** patch of water in the distance. You're so thirsty, you begin to run, but when you reach the pond, it **disappears**. In fact, it was never there at all. What you saw was only a mirage.

Mirages are similar to optical **illusions**. Light waves travel from the sun into Earth's atmosphere. Normally, light moves in a straight line, but the speed varies depending on the **temperature** of the air. In deserts, the ground is often hotter than the air, which causes the air just above it to warm. As light hits this warmer air, it **bends** into a U-shape.

When light bends, it creates a *shimmering effect. To the human eye, this can look like sunlight shining across water. This ____________ occurs because the human brain cannot **register** a bend in light. Instead, we assume the shimmering comes from an object close to the ground. In the desert, this object appears to be the **surface** of water.

▸ Mirages in deserts

▲ A mirage in a cold region

Mirages can also happen when the temperature difference is reversed. In some regions, the temperature close to the ground is colder than the air above it. This causes light from the sun to bend up and project an image above a real object. These mirages are common in colder regions and near oceans. Although they are rare, they can produce **spectacular** images in the sky. **Words 247**

P4 Mirages in __________ regions

*shimmer: to shine with light, often appearing as though the light is waving gently

What is the passage mainly about?

a. Mirages that happen in cold weather
b. Dangers in the desert environment
c. Ways light moves through water
d. How and where mirages happen

Optical Illusions: An optical illusion uses light, color, and patterns to make an image that tricks the brain into thinking it is something else. This occurs because the brain cannot register what the eye is truly seeing.

Reading Comprehension

- **Answer the following questions.**

1 Which is closest in meaning to the word relentless?

a. persistent b. respectful c. inviting d. violent

2 When does light bend in the desert?

a. As it leaves the sun
b. As it hits warmer air
c. As it touches the sand
d. As it turns sideways

3 Which is true according to paragraph 3?

a. Mirages usually only last for a few seconds at a time.
b. Sunlight is primarily responsible for changes in the air.
c. Light bending looks like sunlight shining across water.
d. A mirage will always appear as a pond in the distance.

4 Which is the best choice for the blank?

a. mission b. version c. emotion d. illusion

5 Which is NOT true about mirages seen in colder regions?

a. Light bends up to project an image above an object.
b. The images can be dangerous to passing ships.
c. The temperature close to the ground is colder.
d. These mirages are commonly seen near oceans.

6 How does light normally move?

____

Organizing the Passage

Complete the organizer with the words in the box.

Mirages

Experiencing a Mirage	• You're lost in the desert when you spot a ❶ __________. • The pond disappears, because it was only a mirage.
How Mirages Occur	• In deserts, the hot ground warms the air just above it. • As light hits the warmer air, it ❷ __________ into a U-shape.
What the Human Brain ❸ __________	• The human brain cannot register a bend in light. • We see a shimmering that appears close to the ❹ __________.
Mirages in Colder Regions	• Mirages can also happen when the ground is colder. • Light bends up and ❺ __________ an image above a real object.

pond registers ground projects bends

Summarizing the Passage

Put the following sentences in order to make an appropriate summary. The first sentence is provided.

Mirages occur when the air close to the ground is warmer than the air above it.

_______ This creates a shimmering effect, like sunlight shining across water.

_______ When light hits this warmer air, it bends into a U-shape.

_______ This can also occur in colder regions when temperatures are reversed.

_______ The human brain can't register a bend in light, so we assume it's an object.

Unit 12
Fire Behavior and Weather

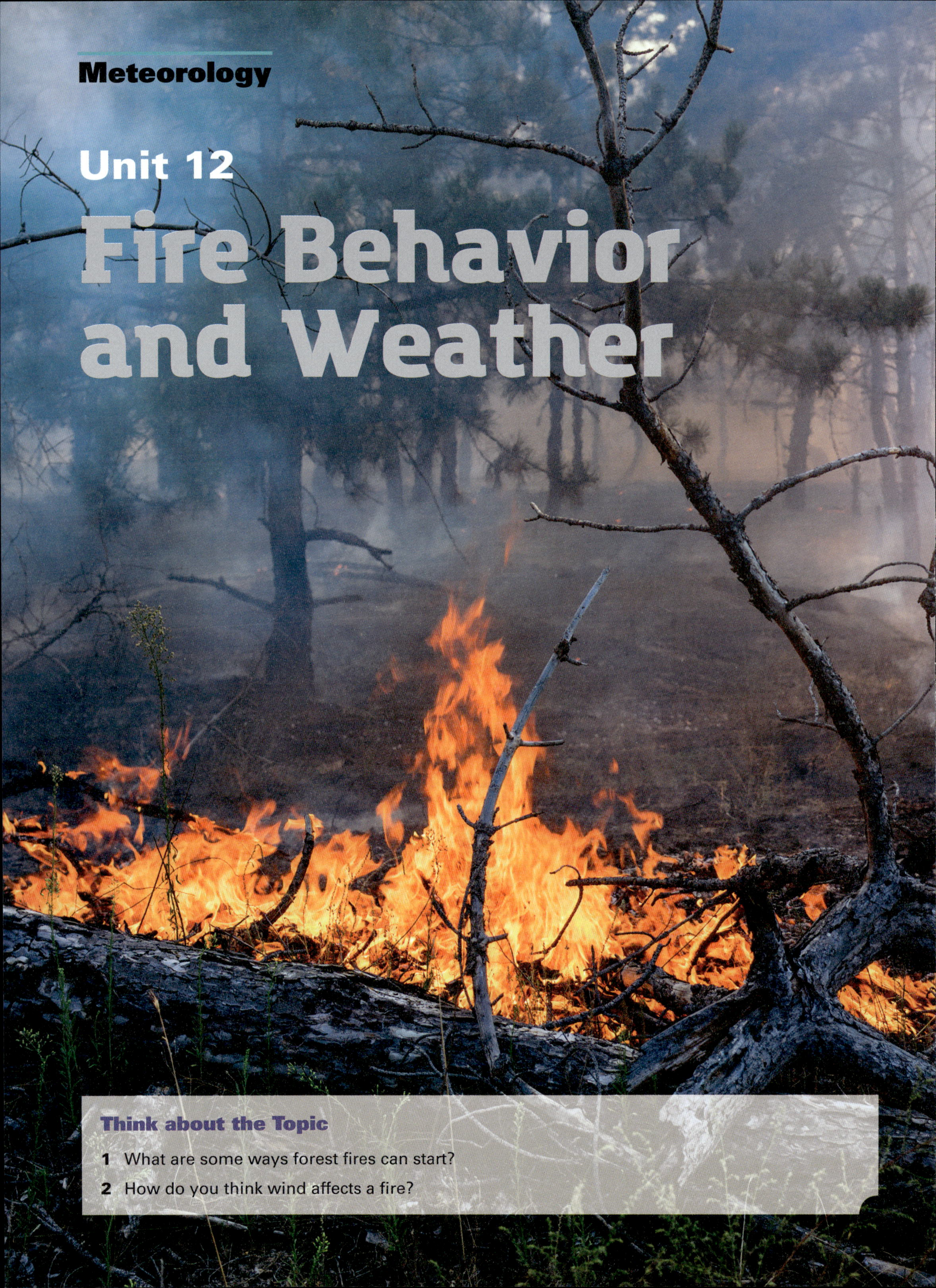

Think about the Topic

1 What are some ways forest fires can start?

2 How do you think wind affects a fire?

Vocabulary Preview

A **Match the words with their definitions by writing the letter in each blank.**

1 mild	______	a. a circumstance or condition
2 factor	______	b. something that can burn easily
3 fuel	______	c. very large
4 enormous	______	d. without stopping
5 steadily	______	e. the amount of resources
6 supply	______	f. the water content found in objects and air
7 abruptly	______	g. not serious
8 moisture	______	h. quickly; without notice

B **Choose the words that have similar** (*sim.*) **or opposite** (*opp.*) **meanings from the box.**

severe	gradually	huge

1 mild ______________ *opp.*

2 enormous ______________ *sim.*

3 abruptly ______________ *opp.*

Background Knowledge

Consequences of Forest Fires:

- Soil:
  - Destroys soil nutrients, making it harder for plants to grow
  - May also cause erosion, which leads to flooding and landslides
- Animal Life:
  - Habitat loss and a decrease in population size
- Atmosphere:
  - An increase of carbon dioxide, which contributes to climate change

Fire Behavior and Weather

Fires are a natural part of forest life. In **mild** cases, fire burns away dying leaves and restores the health of the forest. However, when forest fires rage out of control, they can pose a threat to animal and human life. Entire cities can be lost to the flames. Why does this happen? Certain weather conditions may contribute to the spread of forest fires.

Q

What is each paragraph mainly about?

P2 The effects of ____________ on forest fires

Temperature is one **factor** that affects forest fires. Light from the sun warms the ground and heats the air above the surface. This in turn heats forest **fuels** and can cause them to catch fire. The temperature of the fuels also determines how fast a fire will spread. Warmer fuels will burn more rapidly. This is why fires tend to burn hotter and spread faster in the middle of the day.

P3 The effects of ____________ on forest fires

Wind can also have an **enormous** effect on the spread of a fire. Fires need oxygen to burn **steadily**. Blowing wind can increase a

fire's oxygen **supply**, which causes the fire to grow larger. Wind also fans the fire, essentially moving the flames to other parts of a forest or city. Since the wind often changes direction **abruptly**, this can make the spread of a fire seem unpredictable.

Humidity is one of the most important factors in fire behavior. Humidity refers to the amount of **moisture** in the air. When the air's moisture content is low, the risk of a fire starting increases dramatically. Low humidity tends to dry out a forest's fuels. Drier fuels will burn hotter and faster, increasing the blaze's size.

P4 The effects of ______________ on forest fires

Words 259

Check the main idea of the passage.

a. Weather conditions may affect the spread of fire.
b. Wind has the most serious effect on forest fires.
c. Forest fuels naturally dry out during warmer months.
d. When moisture is present, fires will die out faster.

The Largest Forest Fire in History: The largest forest fire ever recorded took place in Siberia in 2003. At the time, 47 million acres of land burned. The fire created dangerous emissions that harmed Earth's atmosphere.

Reading Comprehension

- **Answer the following questions.**

1 Why does the author mention that entire cities can be lost in paragraph 1?

a. To explain a rare disaster
b. To list the benefits of mild fires
c. To compare cities with forests
d. To stress the danger of a large fire

2 Which is true about forest fuels?

a. Their temperature determines how fast a fire will spread.
b. They heat the air and surrounding plants on warm days.
c. Their size causes wind to change direction abruptly.
d. They commonly cool down in the middle of the day.

3 What does the underlined part in the passage mean?

a. Wind is responsible for a fire getting its fuel supply.
b. An increase in oxygen will create an explosion during a fire.
c. Without an oxygen supply, a fire cannot continue burning.
d. When the oxygen supply is increased, fires begin to die.

4 Which is closest in meaning to the word unpredictable?

a. uncertain b. random c. disturbing d. shocking

5 Which is true about drier fuels?

a. They increase wind speed.
b. They attract more sunlight.
c. They pose less of a threat.
d. They burn hotter and faster.

6 What is humidity?

____

Organizing the Passage

Complete the organizer with the words in the box.

Fire Behavior and Weather

The Effects of Temperature	• Sunlight warms forest ❶ ______________ and causes them to catch fire. • Warmer fuels burn more ❷ ______________, causing fires to spread.
The Effects of Wind	• ❸ ______________ wind can increase a fire's oxygen supply. • Wind also fans the ❹ ______________, moving them to other areas.
The Effects of Humidity	• Low humidity ❺ ______________ a forest's fuels. • This can cause fuels to burn hotter and faster.

rapidly　　dries out　　blowing　　fuels　　flames

Summarizing the Passage

The following is a summary of the passage. Fill in the blanks with the appropriate words.

conditions　　humidity　　spread　　oxygen　　warmer

Certain weather ❶ ______________ can contribute to the spread of forest fires. Temperature is one factor that can affect this spread. Light from the sun warms forest fuels. ❷ ______________ fuels will burn more rapidly. This is why fires tend to burn hotter and ❸ ______________ faster in the middle of the day. Wind can also affect a fire's spread by increasing its ❹ ______________ supply. Wind also fans the flames and can make a fire become unpredictable. ❺ ______________ is one of the most important factors in fire behavior. This means drier fuels tend to burn hotter and faster.

Chapter 7

Biology

Unit 13 Evolving Gut Bacteria

Unit 14 Deep Sea Life

Biology is the study of living organisms. These organisms may be tiny, simple creatures, or they might be large complex species. Biologists study how organisms adapt to their environments and how they interact with each other.

Unit 13

Evolving Gut Bacteria

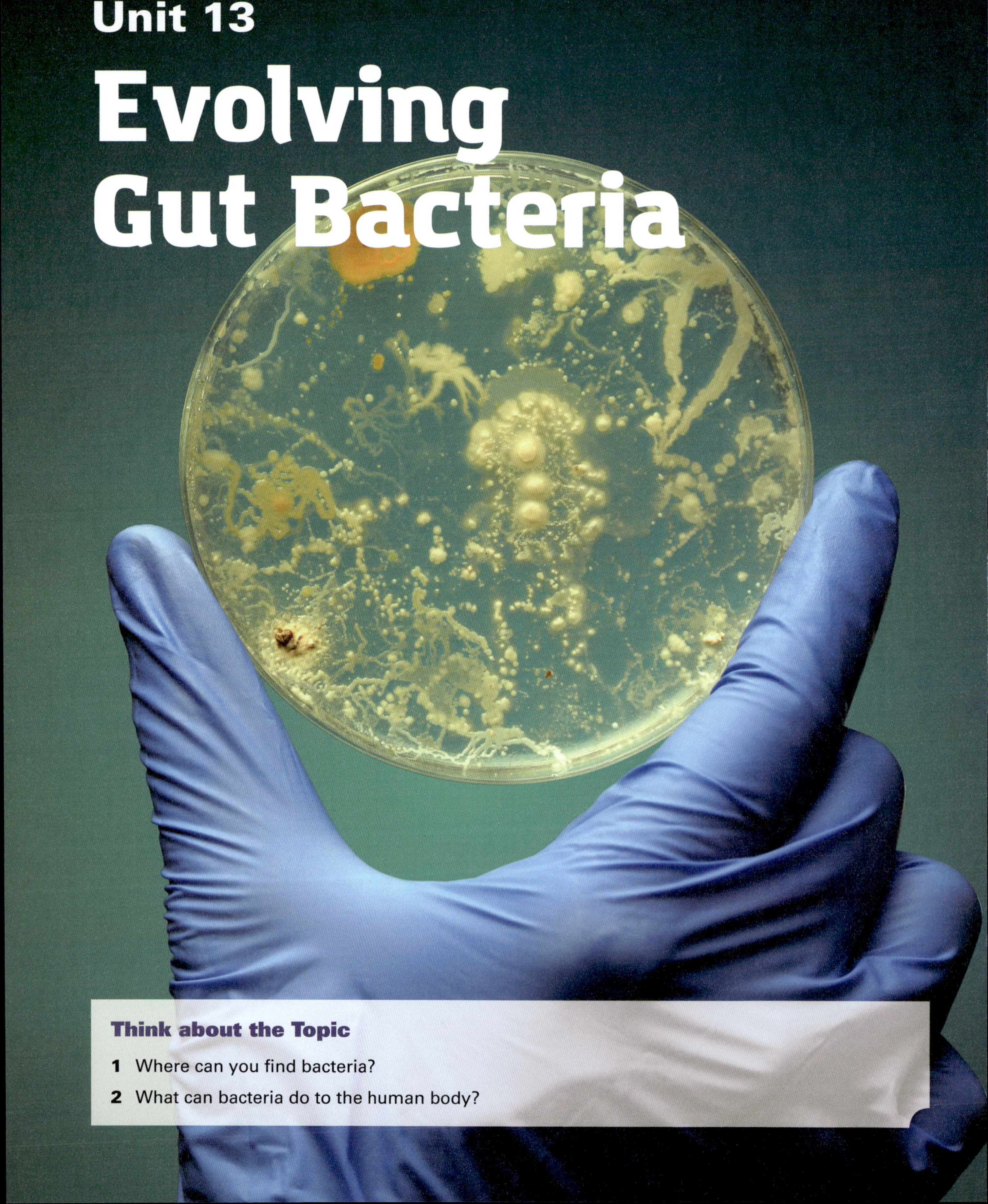

Think about the Topic

1. Where can you find bacteria?
2. What can bacteria do to the human body?

Vocabulary Preview

A **Match the words with their definitions by writing the letter in each blank.**

1 gut ______ a. not sick or injured

2 for instance ______ b. the features of an organism, often found in DNA

3 evolve ______ c. to provide medical care

4 digest ______ d. as an example

5 healthy ______ e. to process food that has been eaten

6 ethnic group ______ f. to change over long periods of time

7 genetics ______ g. a group that shares a common cultural background

8 treat ______ h. the lower part of the intestines

B **Choose the words that have similar** (*sim.*) **or opposite** (*opp.*) **meanings from the box.**

ill	absorb	progress

1 evolve ______ *sim.*

2 digest ______ *sim.*

3 healthy ______ *opp.*

Background Knowledge

Maintaining Healthy Gut Bacteria:

- Avoid:
  - Processed foods and unhealthy fats
  - Antibiotics, which can kill gut bacteria
- Consume:
  - Fiber from fresh vegetables
  - Yogurts, cheeses, and fermented foods like kimchi

Evolving Gut Bacteria

What is each paragraph mainly about?

P1 Healthy ________ bacteria

Bacteria species are often feared, as they can cause many terrible diseases. There are many helpful bacteria species, however. **Gut** bacteria, **for instance**, live inside the intestines. These special bacteria help with digestion. They **evolve** to suit a person's body. In fact, they can evolve very quickly. Why might this occur?

P2 The effects of ________ on gut bacteria

Firstly, a person's diet can affect gut bacteria. **Digesting** fiber is a difficult job. Gut bacteria are useful for this. However, a person might try a new type of fiber. At first, their gut bacteria will have a hard time digesting the fiber. Over time, though, the gut bacteria will change. They will adapt to this new fiber and will soon be able to help with digestion.

P3 Gut bacteria and the ________ system

A person's immune system might also cause gut bacteria to change. The immune system hunts and kills bacteria in the body. This keeps a person **healthy**. But the immune system might also kill gut bacteria. Scientists think gut bacteria change quickly to avoid being killed. The immune system has a hard time noticing new bacteria. Thus, gut bacteria can survive by hiding.

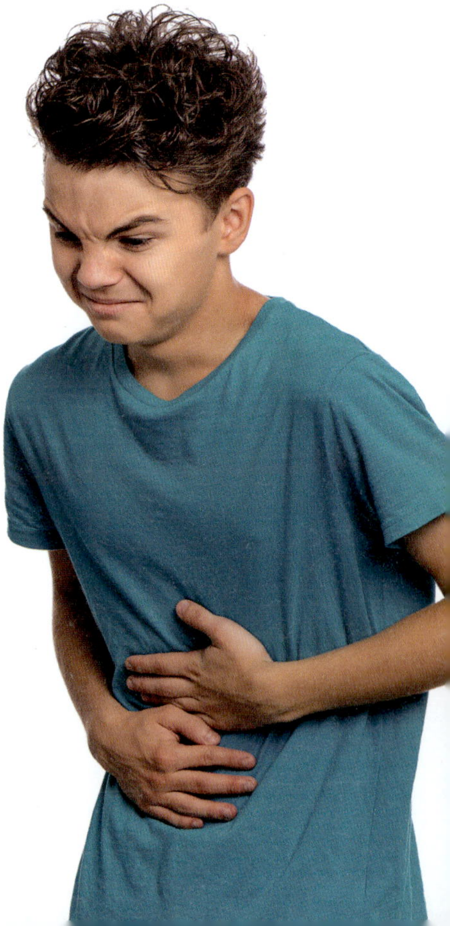

P4 Trends in gut ________ science

Some people have similar gut bacteria. Gender, age, and weight seem to have no effect on these bacteria. But

people of the same **ethnic group** often have similar bacteria. This may be due to **genetics**. It may also be due to shared diet. Scientists hope to continue studying gut bacteria. In the future, gut bacteria could be used to **treat** illnesses. They might also be used to treat digestive problems. Words 250

The Immune System: The immune system defends the body against viruses and bacteria. The immune system will attack and kill these invaders. It might also prevent future infections.

What is the passage mainly about?

a. Improving the gut bacteria in your body
b. How gut bacteria adapt to a person's body
c. Ways the immune system affects digestion
d. The effect of diet on digestion and weight

Reading Comprehension

- **Answer the following questions.**

1 Why are some bacteria species often feared?

a. They cannot live in the body.
b. They fight the signs of aging.
c. They cause terrible diseases.
d. They kill other bacteria species.

2 The word this in the passage refers to

a. a person's diet b. digesting fiber c. special bacteria d. a person's body

3 How do gut bacteria react to new fiber at first?

a They become sick and die.
b. They quickly adapt to it.
c. They immediately reject it.
d. They cannot digest it well.

4 Which is NOT true about the immune system?

a. It has a hard time noticing new bacteria.
b. It hunts and kills bacteria in the body.
c. It helps the body digest unfamiliar foods.
d. It might also kill helpful gut bacteria.

5 Which is true about people who share similar gut bacteria?

a. They use gut bacteria to treat serious illnesses.
b. They have the same gender, age, and weight.
c. They might consume the same types of foods.
d. They regularly try digesting new forms of fiber.

6 How might gut bacteria be used in the future?

Organizing the Passage

Complete the organizer with the words in the box.

Evolving Gut Bacteria

Heathy Gut Bacteria	• There are many helpful bacteria species. • Gut bacteria live inside the body and help with ❶ ______________.
The Effects of ❷ ______________ on Gut Bacteria	• Gut bacteria have a hard time digesting new fiber. • Over time, they ❸ ______________ to this new fiber.
Gut Bacteria and the Immune System	• The immune system hunts and kills bacteria in the body. • Gut ❹ ______________ change quickly to avoid being killed.
Trends in Gut Bacteria Science	• People of the same ethnic group have similar bacteria. • Gut bacteria could one day be used to ❺ ______________ diseases.

digestion	treat	bacteria	adapt	diet

Summarizing the Passage

Put the following sentences in order to make an appropriate summary. The first sentence is provided.

There are many helpful bacteria species, such as gut bacteria.

______ Gut bacteria can evolve quickly to suit a person's body.

______ In the future, gut bacteria could be used to treat illnesses and digestive problems.

______ Over time, gut bacteria will adapt to changes in a person's diet.

______ Gut bacteria will also change in order to hide from the immune system.

Biology

Unit 14

Deep Sea Life

Think about the Topic

1. Name some animals that live in the ocean.
2. What can survive deep in the ocean?

Vocabulary Preview

A **Match the words with their definitions by writing the letter in each blank.**

1 extreme ______ a. something that is used to attract an animal

2 depth ______ b. the facial bones that hold the teeth

3 pressure ______ c. one part of many

4 jaw ______ d. to remain unaffected by a force

5 segment ______ e. reaching a high degree

6 withstand ______ f. the distance from the surface to the bottom

7 sense *(n.)* ______ g. a force on an object, caused by water, air, etc

8 lure *(n.)* ______ h. a way something is observed; sight, sound, taste, touch, smell

B **Choose the words that have similar** *(sim.)* **or opposite** *(opp.)* **meanings from the box.**

resist	section	slight

1 extreme ______________ *opp.*

2 segment ______________ *sim.*

3 withstand ______________ *sim.*

Background Knowledge

The Depth of the Ocean:

On average, the ocean floor is just over 3,600 meters below the water's surface. However, the deepest part of the ocean is called the Challenger Deep. This is a trench that stretches for several hundred kilometers near Guam. It was discovered in 1875 and is over 10,000 meters deep.

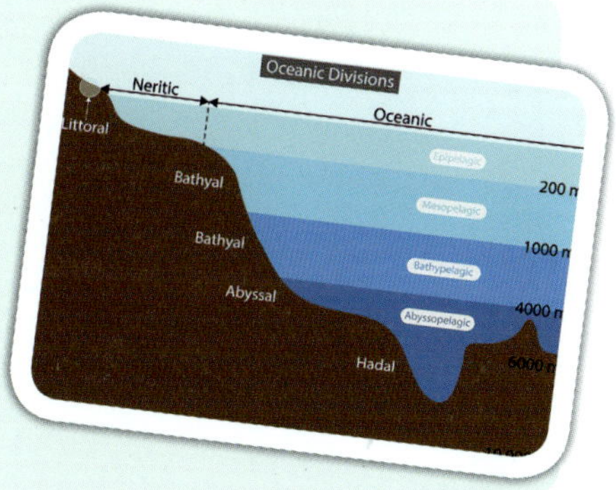

Deep Sea Life

What is each paragraph mainly about?

P1 The deep-sea (creature / environment)

P2 The giant ____________

P3 The ____________ shark

The oceans are harsh environments. Sea creatures must adapt to **extreme** conditions to survive. The lower the **depth**, the harsher the environment. There is very little oxygen or food in the deep sea. The **pressure** there is very high, and the water is extremely cold. Some unique creatures, however, can survive in these conditions.

The giant isopod lives in the Pacific and Atlantic oceans. This creature has four sets of **jaws**. Its body has seven **segments** with numerous legs for walking and swimming. It's about 75 centimeters long and can be found 2,400 meters below the surface. There, it feeds on dead sea creatures, such as whales, fish, and squid. The giant isopod has adapted to **withstand** the cold temperature and high pressure.

The great hammerhead shark also lives in the deep sea. It swims in depths of 600 meters and grows to be over 5 meters long. This species is known for its hammer-shaped head. This shape helps it see its prey better. Since little sunlight reaches the deep sea, this predator needs to have excellent **senses**. However, the great hammerhead shark will sometimes eat other hammerhead sharks.

▲ A great hammerhead shark

▲ A giant isopod

The anglerfish is another unique deep-sea creature. This fish is only about 18 centimeters long, but it lives at depths of at least 2,000 meters. Sunlight is completely absent there, which makes it difficult for fish to attract prey. Thus, the anglerfish has a special **lure**. This lure is attached to its head and is filled with light-producing bacteria. The anglerfish shines this light to attract prey. Words 256

P4 The ____________

Check the main idea of the passage.

a. Oceans are harsh environments that no creature can live in.
b. Some unique sea creatures can survive deep in the ocean.
c. The giant isopod is the only species found in the deep sea.
d. Dangerous sea creatures use special methods to lure prey.

i **Remotely Operated Vehicles**: Remotely operated vehicles are small machines that can travel deep into the sea. A driver operates the vehicle from the surface using a remote. These vehicles help humans explore the deep sea.

Reading Comprehension

- **Answer the following questions.**

1 What does the underlined part in the passage mean?

a. Sea creatures prefer the harsh environment of the sea.
b. There is very little oxygen found deep in ocean waters.
c. It is not possible for humans to survive at extreme depths.
d. The ocean environment becomes more extreme with depth.

2 Which is NOT true about the giant isopod?

a. It feeds on dead sea creatures, like whales.
b. It has four sets of jaws and numerous legs.
c. It is 75 centimeters with seven segments.
d. It has adapted to withstand low pressures.

3 Why does the author mention the shark's hammer-shaped head in paragraph 3?

a. To mention why the shark needs sunlight
b. To explain how this animal finds its prey
c. To compare it with more deadly sharks
d. To note a feature common in deep-sea life

4 Which is true about hammerhead sharks?

a. They have special noses to smell their prey.
b. They cannot see well in brightly lit seawater.
c. They can grow to be over 18 meters in length.
d. They sometimes eat other hammerhead sharks.

5 What can you guess about anglerfish prey?

a. They create and shine their own light.
b. They live at depths of 2,000 meters.
c. They are mostly bacteria species.
d. They are attracted to sunlight.

6 What is an anglerfish lure filled with?

____

Organizing the Passage

Complete the organizer with the words in the box.

Deep Sea Life

The Deep-Sea Environment	• There is very little ❶ ______________ or food. • The ❷ ______________ is high, and the water is extremely cold.
The Giant Isopod	• It can be found 2,400 meters below the ❸ __________. • It has adapted to the temperature and pressure.
The Hammerhead ❹ ______________	• It swims in depths of 600 meters in the ocean. • With little sunlight, it needs to have excellent senses.
The Anglerfish	• It has a special lure filled with light-producing bacteria. • It shines the light, and ❺ ______________ are attracted to it.

shark   pressure   prey   surface   oxygen

Summarizing the Passage

The following is a summary of the passage. Fill in the blanks with the appropriate words.

senses   anglerfish   squid   lure   harsh

The oceans are ❶ ______________ environments, but some creatures can survive in extreme conditions. The giant isopod can be found 2,400 meters below the surface. There, it feeds on dead sea creatures, such as whales, fish, and ❷ ______________. The hammerhead shark swims in depths of 600 meters. Its hammer-shaped head helps it see prey better. It must also have excellent ❸ ______________. The ❹ ______________ lives at depths of at least 2,000 meters. Sunlight is absent, so the anglerfish uses a ❺ ____________ to attract its prey.

Chapter 8
Arts

Unit 15 Ventriloquism

Unit 16 African Cave Art

Art is an expression of human creativity. This creativity may be expressed visually, such as in painting or sculpture. It might also be performance-based, such as dance, drama, or music. Artists share their ideas and make social commentary through their creations.

Unit 15
Ventriloquism

Think about the Topic

1 How might a performer use puppets?

2 What does a ventriloquist do?

Vocabulary Preview

A **Match the words with their definitions by writing the letter in each blank.**

1 religious	______	a. a traveling festival
2 oracle	______	b. someone who tells the future
3 prediction	______	c. to begin again; to make new again
4 witchcraft	______	d. having to do with a religion
5 carnival	______	e. a contest of skill
6 competition	______	f. a guess about the future
7 renew	______	g. the state of wanting to know more about something
8 interest	______	h. magic done by a witch

B **Choose the words that have similar** (*sim.*) **or opposite** (*opp.*) **meanings from the box.**

contest	prophet	fair

1 oracle ______________ *sim.*

2 competition ______________ *sim.*

3 carnival ______________ *sim.*

Background Knowledge

Ventriloquist Dummies:

A ventriloquist dummy is the doll a ventriloquist uses during a stage performance. Traditionally, the dolls looked like small humans. Their faces were brightly painted so audiences could see them better. Today, however, some ventriloquists prefer to use dummies that look more like cartoon characters and animals.

Ventriloquism

Q

What is each paragraph mainly about?

P1 Ventriloquism in ancient ______________

P2 Ventriloquism in the ______________ Ages

P3 Ventriloquism in the ______________

Modern ventriloquists are known as stage performers. But the first ventriloquists were actually much different. In fact, early ventriloquism was a **religious** practice. The ancient Greeks believed the dead lived inside the human stomach. When the stomach made noises, it was the dead speaking. The dead could tell the future. **Oracles** listened to the noises and made **predictions**.

By the Middle Ages, opinions about ventriloquism had changed. It was no longer seen as a religious practice. Instead, it was considered a form of **witchcraft**. Christians thought ventriloquists could talk to the dead. This idea went against their religion. Thus, anyone who performed was considered a witch. Witches were often caught and executed.

In the 1800s, ventriloquism became a form of entertainment. Ventriloquists traveled with **carnivals** and performed on stages. During a performance, a ventriloquist would throw his voice. This means he would speak without moving his lips. ❶ It sounded as though his voice was coming from somewhere else. ❷ Eventually, ventriloquists began using dolls. ❸ A ventriloquist created a special voice for each of his dummies. ❹

▲ Ventriloquist Paul Zerdin © Debby Wong

▲ Ventriloquist Darci Lynne Farmer © lev radin

P4 (Talent competitions / Ventriloquism) in modern times

Ventriloquism lost popularity in the 20th century. By 2010, there were very few ventriloquists. However, some ventriloquists competed in talent **competitions**. This **renewed** the public's **interest** in ventriloquism. Darci Lynne Farmer made history in 2017. She was the first child ventriloquist to win *America's Got Talent*. This inspired many to learn the art of ventriloquism. **Words 233**

The Most Famous Ventriloquist in the 20th Century: Edgar Bergon was the most famous ventriloquist of the 20th century. He named his dummy Charlie McCarthy. Bergen and his dummy appeared on stage, in film, and even on the radio.

What is the passage mainly about?

a. Ventriloquism and witchcraft in the Middle Ages
b. The history and development of ventriloquism
c. How ventriloquism became popular on talent shows
d. The first ventriloquist performances with dummies

Reading Comprehension

- **Answer the following questions.**

1 **Which is NOT true about the dead according to ancient Greek beliefs?**

a. They lived inside the stomach.
b. They could predict the future.
c. They could practice witchcraft.
d. They made noises in the stomach

2 **What happened to witches in the Middle Ages?**

a. They became Christians.
b. They predicted the future.
c. They performed at carnivals.
d. They were caught and executed.

3 **Which is true about ventriloquists according to paragraph 3?**

a. They designed their own dummies.
b. They spoke without moving their lips.
c. They were accused of being witches.
d. They competed in talent competitions.

4 **Where would the following sentence best fit in the passage?**

These were called dummies.

a. ❶ b. ❷ c. ❸ d. ❹

5 **What does the word This in paragraph 4 refer to?**

a. Ventriloquists traveling with carnivals
b. A ventriloquist creating special voices
c. Ventriloquists competing in competitions
d. Darci Lynne Farmer winning a competition

6 **What happened to ventriloquism in the 20th century?**

____

Organizing the Passage

Complete the organizer with the words in the box.

Ventriloquism

In Ancient ❶ ______	• It was believed that the dead lived inside the stomach. • Oracles listened to stomach noises and made predictions.
In the Middle Ages	• Ventriloquism was considered a form of witchcraft. • Witches were often caught and ❷ ______.
In the 1800s	• Ventriloquism became a form of stage ❸ ______. • Later, ventriloquists used dolls called ❹ ______.
In Modern Times	• Ventriloquism steadily lost popularity over the years. • Talent ❺ ______ renewed the public's interest.

competitions   dummies   entertainment   executed   Greece

Summarizing the Passage

Put the following sentences in order to make an appropriate summary. The first sentence is provided.

Modern ventriloquism is a stage performance, but it wasn't always this way.

______ Ventriloquism lost popularity, but recent talent competitions renewed interest.

______ By the Middle Ages, ventriloquism was considered a form of witchcraft.

______ In the 1800s, ventriloquists traveled with carnivals and performed on stages.

______ In ancient Greece, ventriloquism was a religious practice done by oracles.

Unit 16

African Cave Art

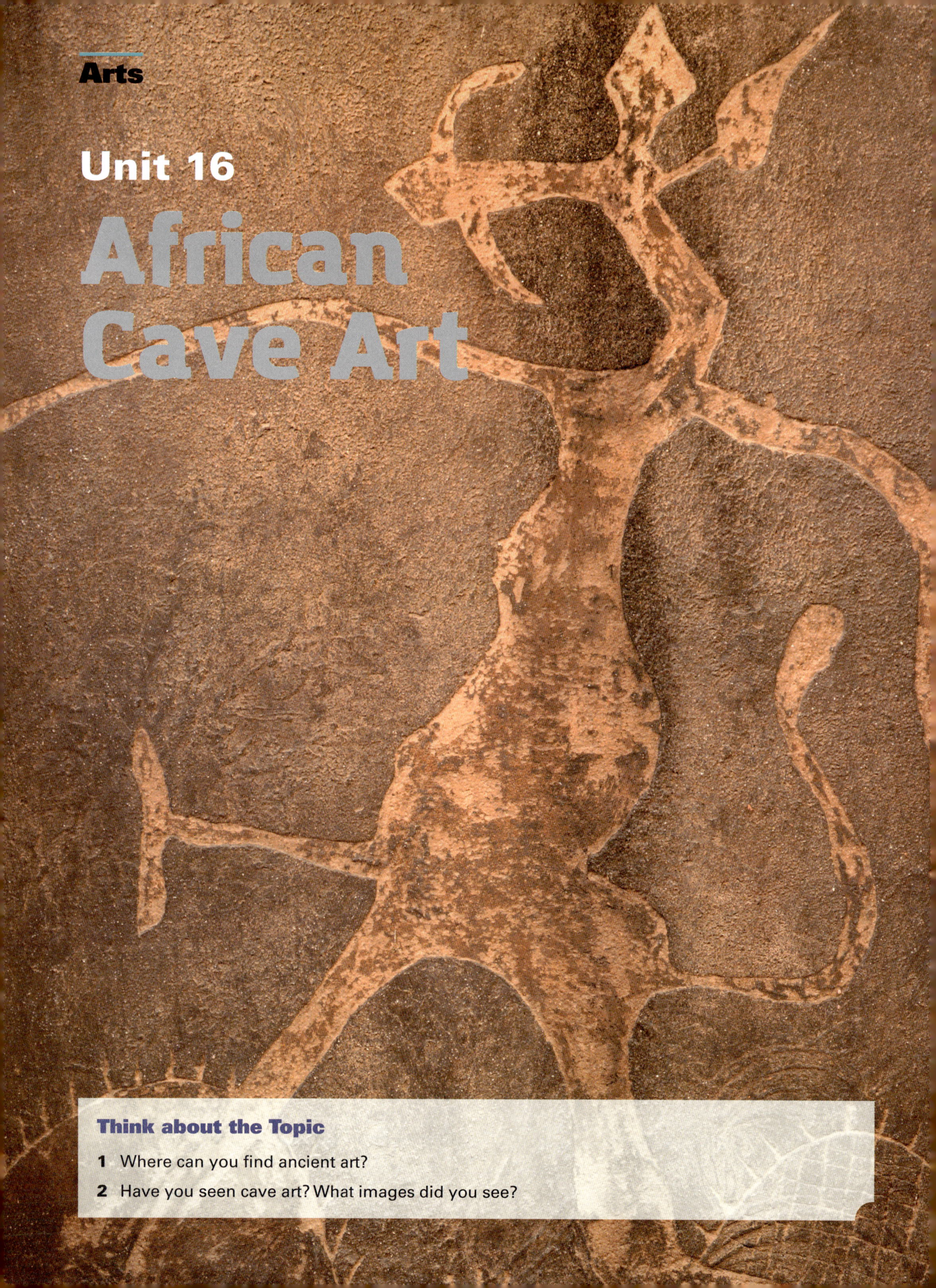

Think about the Topic

1 Where can you find ancient art?

2 Have you seen cave art? What images did you see?

Vocabulary Preview

A **Match the words with their definitions by writing the letter in each blank.**

1 prize *(v.)*	______	a. kept in good condition
2 continent	______	b. to have been made at a certain time in the past
3 well-preserved	______	c. a landmass often containing more than one country
4 pattern	______	d. close to the present
5 recent	______	e. to value highly
6 herder	______	f. a design of repeating lines or shapes
7 date back to	______	g. to move from one area to another, often seasonal
8 migrate	______	h. a person who looks after and moves animals

B **Choose the words that have similar** *(sim.)* **or opposite** *(opp.)* **meanings from the box.**

journey	treasure	ancient

1 prize ______________ *sim.*

2 recent ______________ *opp.*

3 migrate ______________ *sim.*

Background Knowledge

Cave Art in Egypt:

- The Cave of Swimmers:
  - Discovered in 1933 by a Hungarian explorer
  - Features images of people swimming
- The Cave of Beasts:
  - Discovered in 2002 by archaeologists
  - Contains over 5,000 figures of humans and animals
  - Also contains hundreds of hand stencils

African Cave Art

Like all societies, early humans **prized** art. The lives of hunter-gatherers were focused mainly on animals. Thus, they often drew images to reflect this. Many early human societies painted on the walls of caves. This type of art can be found on most **continents**. However, Africa boasts some of the most **well-preserved** cave art on the planet.

Q What is each paragraph mainly about?

P2 Art of the Apollo 11 ____________

The Apollo 11 cave contains some of the oldest art ever found. Located in Namibia, this cave features mostly *geometric **patterns**. The paintings may have been created up to 27,500 years ago. However, the oldest known rock painting was discovered in South Africa. This rock features lines drawn with an *ochre crayon. It's estimated to be 73,000 years old.

▲ Paintings in the Laas Geel cave

P3 More (recent / numerous) cave art

Africa is rich with more **recent** cave art as well. The Laas Geel cave was discovered in Somaliland. French archaeologists found this cave in 2002. It contains numerous paintings of wild animals, cattle, and **herders**. These paintings may have been created around 5,000 years ago. More cave art was discovered in this region in 2008. These images, however, feature hunters on horseback and **date back to** 3000 BC.

▲ Paintings in Tassili n'Ajjer in Algeria

The most well-preserved cave art can be found in North Africa. Caves in Algeria, for example, contain more than 15,000 different images. These paintings show **migrating** animals as well as changes in the weather. Some of them date back to 6000 BC. Similarly, the Cave of Swimmers and the Cave of Beasts are both located in Egypt. These incredible caves contain thousands of well-preserved paintings. **Words 249**

P4 The most ______________ cave art

*geometric: describes a style of art that uses straight lines or shapes

*ochre: a pigment made of clay, usually yellow, red, or brown

i **Cave Art Around the World:** Cave art can be found on nearly every continent. Some of the most spectacular cave art is located in Europe. The Lascaux Caves in France, for example, have some of the most impressive cave art in the world.

What is the passage mainly about?

a. Cave art found throughout Africa
b. A special cave found in North Africa
c. How cave art was painted on rock
d. The oldest cave art in the world

Reading Comprehension

- **Choose the best answers.**

1 The word they in the passage refers to

a. lives
b. animals
c. all societies
d. hunter-gatherers

2 Which is true about the Apollo 11 cave?

a. Its art may have been made 27,500 years ago.
b. It was discovered in Somaliland by archaeologists.
c. It contains the most well-preserved art in Africa.
d. The paintings mostly show migrating animals.

3 What does the oldest known rock painting feature?

a. Numerous geometric patterns
b. Lines drawn with an ochre crayon
c. Wild animals, cattle, and herders
d. Hunters shown on horseback

4 Why does the author mention North Africa?

a. To note where the best-preserved cave art is
b. To compare caves in two different countries
c. To name the location of the oldest cave art
d. To explain how the first caves were found

5 Which is closest in meaning to the word incredible?

a. harmonious
b. unbelievable
c. defective
d. attractive

6 When did archaeologists find the Laas Geel cave?

Organizing the Passage

Complete the organizer with the words in the box.

African Cave Art

Art of the Apollo 11 Cave	• It is located in Namibia and features geometric ❶ ________________. • It ❷ ________________ some of the oldest art ever found.
More Recent Cave Art	• More recent art was found in 2002 and 2008. • This art shows animals, herders, and ❸ ________________ on horseback.
The Most ❹ ________________ Cave Art	• Caves in Algeria contain 15,000 different images. • Thousands of well-preserved images can be seen in ❺ ________________.

patterns　　well-preserved　　contains　　hunters　　Egypt

Summarizing the Passage

The following is a summary of the passage. Fill in the blanks with the appropriate words.

boasts　　recent　　humans　　discovered　　horseback

Many early ❶ ________________ painted on the walls of caves. Africa ❷ ________________ some of the most well-preserved cave art on the planet. The Apollo 11 cave, located in Namibia, contains some of the oldest art ever found. However, the oldest rock painting was ❸ ________________ in South Africa. Africa is also rich with more ❹ ________________ art. Archaeologists have discovered numerous paintings of animals, herders, and hunters on ❺ ________________. The most well-preserved cave art can be found in North Africa. Caves in Algeria and Egypt contain thousands of incredible images.

TOEFL
Practice Test

Marsupials

Marsupials are unique mammals commonly found in Australia. These animals vary greatly in appearance. Some are quite large and walk on two legs while others are good climbers, using all four legs. However, most marsupials have a common feature: they have a pouch to carry their young in.

When marsupials give birth, their young are extremely small and underdeveloped. These babies crawl into their mother's pouch. The pouch is made up of skin folds and fur. It can be located on the mother's abdomen or on her back. The young stay in this protective pouch for many weeks. There, they consume the mother's milk and grow large enough to survive in the wild on their own.

Kangaroos are perhaps the most famous marsupials. Native to Australia, these animals have powerful hind legs. Since they walk upright, their pouches are found on their abdomens. Their young are born when they are very small, only about the size of a bean. A baby kangaroo will crawl into its mother's pouch and remain there for up to nine months. After the baby leaves the pouch, it will continue to drink the mother's milk for nine additional months.

A lesser-known marsupial is the opossum. Opossums look similar to rodents with rounded ears and pointed noses. Generally, they live and care for their young in trees. Opossums give birth to up to 20 babies at one time. Each baby is about the size of a jelly bean. It develops inside its mother's pouch, and when it is older, the mother will carry it on her back.

1 **Which of the following sentences best expresses the essential information in the highlighted sentence in the passage? Incorrect answer choices change the meaning in important ways or leave out essential information.**

Some are quite large and walk on two legs while others are good climbers, using all four legs.

Ⓐ The best-known marsupials are extremely large and walk on two back legs.

Ⓑ Most small marsupials are better at climbing than they are at walking upright.

Ⓒ All large marsupials walk on two legs, but some also use their front legs.

Ⓓ Some large marsupials walk on two legs, but others use all four for climbing.

2 **The word "protective" in the passage is closest in meaning to**

Ⓐ safe
Ⓑ certain
Ⓒ vibrant
Ⓓ closed

3 **The author's description of kangaroos mentions which of the following?**

Ⓐ A rodent-like appearance with rounded ears
Ⓑ Folds of skin and fur located on the back
Ⓒ A pouch located on the mother's abdomen
Ⓓ Four powerful legs for climbing up trees

4 **Why does the author mention "a jelly bean" in paragraph 4?**

Ⓐ To describe the size of a 9-month-old baby opossum
Ⓑ To express how underdeveloped baby opossums are
Ⓒ To elaborate on the common diet of adult opossums
Ⓓ To compare the sizes of two well-known marsupials

5 **The word "it" in the passage refers to**

Ⓐ the mother's milk
Ⓑ the mother's pouch
Ⓒ each baby
Ⓓ a jelly bean

6 **An introductory sentence for a brief summary of the passage is provided below. Complete the summary by selecting the THREE answer choices that express the most important ideas of the passage. Some sentences do not belong because they express ideas that are not presented in the passage or are minor ideas in the passage.**

Marsupials are unique animals that carry their young in pouches.

1. A baby kangaroo crawls into its mother's pouch and stays there for nine months.
2. Most marsupials are native to Australia, but much of their habitat is endangered.
3. The opossum is a lesser-known marsupial that uses all four legs for climbing trees.
4. When marsupial babies are born, they are extremely small and underdeveloped.
5. Baby opossums develop inside a pouch and then are carried on the mother's back.

TOEFL Practice Test ❷

Jupiter's Moons

Jupiter is the largest planet in the solar system. Numerous moons can be found orbiting this enormous gas giant. In fact, Jupiter has so many moons that not all of them have been named. Scientists think there are currently about 79 moons. However, the largest four have garnered the most interest.

Jupiter's four largest moons are known as the Galilean moons. They were named after Italian astronomer Galileo Galilei. He discovered these moons in 1610. At first, he thought he was looking at stars. However, these objects were moving. Galileo determined that these were moons. They were the first discovered beyond Earth's moon.

Ganymede is the largest Galilean moon. Surprisingly, this moon is even larger than the planet Mercury. Ganymede is special among moons. No other moon has its own magnetic field. Although it is smaller, Callisto is still considered significant. Callisto's rocky surface is covered in craters. These craters are very old. They show the history of the solar system.

Io is the hottest of Jupiter's moons. This moon has more volcanic activity than any moon or planet in the solar system. Its high heat makes it impossible for water to form on its surface. Europa, on the other hand, is mostly covered in ice. Scientists think this ice could be covering an ocean. Europa might have twice as much water as Earth. This makes the moon particularly interesting. Since water is needed to sustain life, there could be alien life below the surface.

1 The word "garnered" in the passage is closest in meaning to

Ⓐ locked
Ⓑ revoked
Ⓒ gathered
Ⓓ transferred

2 According to the passage, which of the following is true about Galileo?

Ⓐ He thought the moons were stars at first.
Ⓑ He discovered all of Jupiter's 79 moons.
Ⓒ He noticed that Europa's surface has ice.
Ⓓ He was the first to study Earth's moon.

3 **The author's description of Callisto mentions all of the following EXCEPT:**

Ⓐ It experiences times of high volcanic activity.
Ⓑ Its surface shows the history of the solar system.
Ⓒ It is considered significant among Jupiter's moons.
Ⓓ It is a rocky moon that is smaller than Ganymede.

4 **According to paragraph 4, water cannot form on Io because**

Ⓐ Jupiter makes volcanoes erupt
Ⓑ it is located too close to the sun
Ⓒ its surface temperature is too high
Ⓓ only ice forms on the planet's surface

5 **The author implies that alien life**

Ⓐ could live on Ganymede and Io
Ⓑ cannot exist in the universe today
Ⓒ has been found in Europa's ocean
Ⓓ consumes water to live and grow

6 **An introductory sentence for a brief summary of the passage is provided below. Complete the summary by selecting the THREE answer choices that express the most important ideas of the passage. Some sentences do not belong because they express ideas that are not presented in the passage or are minor ideas in the passage.**

Jupiter has numerous moons, but the four largest have attracted the most attention.

❶ Ganymede has its own magnetic field, and Callisto is covered in craters.
❷ Europa may be covered in ice, but it could also have several oceans.
❸ Galileo Galilei discovered the Galilean moons, Jupiter's four largest, in 1610.
❹ At first, Galileo thought he was looking at an image of the stars in space.
❺ Io is the hottest of Jupiter's moons while Europa is mostly covered in ice.

TOEFL Practice Test ❸

Film Adaptation

Film adaptation is the process of changing a written work to a visual one. Film companies produce many adaptations each year. Some are considered more successful than others. Books are often chosen as source material. However, film companies also choose stage plays and even comic books.

Novels are often adapted into films. Film companies select a popular novel and then hire a screenwriter. This writer creates a screenplay based on the book. [1] Novels are much longer than screenplays. [2] This means some of the story cannot be included in the film. [3] Screenwriters must make important choices about what to include. [4]

Many stage plays are also adapted for the big screen. A play's script looks similar to a screenplay. This makes adapting it easier. However, screenwriters still need to make important decisions. They often change plot points or omit characters. Sometimes, the play is quite old. For example, Shakespearean plays are frequently made into films. Some screenwriters stay true to the story. Others make drastic changes. They might change the setting. They might even include more modern language.

In recent years, more and more comic books have been adapted into films. Comic books, such as those published by Marvel, are full of exciting characters. These characters go on many adventures. Films are not long enough to include everything. Screenwriters must decide what to change. Drastic changes may upset fans, however. Thus, there is often a team of screenwriters. These writers work together to create the best possible story.

1 **According to paragraph 1, which of the following is true about film adaptations?**

Ⓐ Book adaptations are the most famous.
Ⓑ Some are more successful than others.
Ⓒ Stage plays are the best source material.
Ⓓ Comic books are rarely adapted to film.

2 **According to paragraph 2, screenwriters must make important choices because**

Ⓐ setting and language should be updated
Ⓑ all of the story needs to be included
Ⓒ novels are much longer than screenplays
Ⓓ fans want to see many new characters

3 **The word "it" in the passage refers to**

Ⓐ a film company

Ⓑ the big screen

Ⓒ a play's script

Ⓓ a screenplay

4 **Which of the following can be inferred about Marvel?**

Ⓐ Marvel has the most exciting comic book characters.

Ⓑ Marvel comics have been adapted for the big screen.

Ⓒ Marvel will likely produce stage plays in the future.

Ⓓ Marvel novels are too long to be made into films.

5 **Look at the four squares [■] that indicate where the following sentence could be added to the passage.**

They may cut characters or change the plot.

Where would the sentence best fit?

6 **An introductory sentence for a brief summary of the passage is provided below. Complete the summary by selecting the THREE answer choices that express the most important ideas of the passage. Some sentences do not belong because they express ideas that are not presented in the passage or are minor ideas in the passage.**

Film companies often adapt novels, stage plays, and comic books into films.

❶ Stage plays are easier to adapt because they look similar to screenplays.

❷ More and more, comic books have been adapted for the big screen in recent years.

❸ Since novels are longer than screenplays, some of the story cannot be included.

❹ Comic books are full of exciting characters that go on many adventures.

❺ Writers work together as a team to create exciting novels and comic books.

TOEFL Practice Test ❹

Water Purification

Humans need fresh water to survive. However, there are many *contaminants in fresh water. It is important to purify water before drinking it. Boiling is the oldest purification method. Heating water can kill the germs inside it. This helps us to avoid getting sick, but it is not always effective. Nowadays, there are more effective ways to purify water.

Filtration is a quick way to purify water. Filtration systems use numerous filters. Water is pumped through the filters. The filters catch contaminants. These include germs and chemicals. Very little water is lost during this process, and the remaining water is safe and clean. Filtration systems can be installed in homes. They are often inexpensive and easy to use. They also do not require a lot of energy to run.

Distillation is another purification method. Unlike filtration, it uses heat. In this system, water is heated to a boil. It is then collected as a vapor. The vapor cools and changes back into a liquid. However, the contaminants are no longer present. This occurs because water boils faster than the contaminants. The clean water vapor rises, leaving behind the germs and chemicals. Once it has been cooled, the water is safe for drinking.

Chlorination is common in cities. Chlorine is a very powerful chemical that can easily kill germs and parasites. Thus, many water treatment plants use it to clean the city's water supply. The water is then pumped into homes, but it may have a chemical taste. As a result, many people choose to filter the water before drinking it.

*contaminant: a substance that pollutes larger substances, such as air, water, or food

1 The word "effective" in the passage is closest in meaning to

Ⓐ surprising
Ⓑ successful
Ⓒ detailed
Ⓓ informed

2 The author's description of filtration mentions all of the following EXCEPT:

Ⓐ Systems are cheap to install and run.
Ⓑ It is the oldest method of purification.
Ⓒ Filters catch germs and chemicals.
Ⓓ Very little water is lost in the process.

3 **The word "It" in the passage refers to**

Ⓐ Method

Ⓑ Heat

Ⓒ System

Ⓓ Water

4 **According to paragraph 3, germs are left behind because**

Ⓐ water boils faster than contaminants

Ⓑ germs die in high temperatures

Ⓒ chemicals are not able to boil

Ⓓ chlorine pushes germs away

5 **Why does the author mention "water treatment plants" in paragraph 4?**

Ⓐ To describe a new development in cities

Ⓑ To recommend a home purification method

Ⓒ To explain why some people filter their water

Ⓓ To stress how effective chlorine is as purifier

6 **An introductory sentence for a brief summary of the passage is provided below. Complete the summary by selecting the THREE answer choices that express the most important ideas of the passage. Some sentences do not belong because they express ideas that are not presented in the passage or are minor ideas in the passage.**

There are currently many effective ways to purify drinking water.

1. Distillation uses heat to boil water, then collects the contaminant-free vapor.
2. Boiling water is the oldest and most effective way to purify drinking water.
3. Filtration systems use filters to catch contaminants, such as germs and chemicals.
4. Chlorination kills germs and parasites before water is pumped into homes.
5. Once water is completely cooled, it is considered safe for drinking.

MEMO

MEMO

MEMO

Building Background Knowledge for Academic Subjects

Fundamental Reading

Rachel Somer

Workbook

BASIC 2

DARAKWON

Building Background Knowledge for Academic Subjects

Fundamental Reading

Rachel Somer

Workbook

BASIC 2

DARAKWON

Unit 1 Healthy Plant Skins

Vocabulary

A Match the words with their correct meanings.

consume	essential	packed with	fiber	maintain

1 very important or necessary ____________

2 being full of something ____________

3 plant material that is difficult to digest ____________

4 to keep the same ____________

5 to eat or drink ____________

B Choose the words from the box to complete the sentences.

pesticides	texture	fiber	peel

1 Doctors recommend eating plenty of ____________.

2 The farmer sprayed ____________ on the vegetables.

3 Some people dislike the ____________ of mushrooms.

4 ____________ the bananas and then chop them into pieces.

Translation

C Read the sentences and translate them into your language.

1 Plants provide us with some of the healthiest foods on the planet.

→ ____________

2 Eating these skins can increase our vitamin and mineral intake.

→ ____________

3 As a result, we are less likely to snack in between meals.

→ ____________

Paraphrasing

D Paraphrase the sentences from the passage with the words in the box.

likewise	exterior	full of	healthy
consume	important	sustain	

1 Vitamins and nutrients are essential for good health.

→ Vitamins and nutrients are very ______________ in order to stay ______________.

2 Fruits like bananas, oranges, and grapefruit have a tough outer skin.

→ Some fruits, such as bananas, oranges, and grapefruit, have a hard ______________.

3 Similarly, potato skins are packed with vitamin C and various minerals.

→ ______________, potato skins are ______________ vitamin C and numerous minerals.

4 People who eat a lot of fiber have an easier time maintaining a healthy weight.

→ Those who ______________ a lot of fiber find it easier to ______________ a healthy weight.

Listening

E Listen to the summary and fill in the blanks.

Plants give us vitamins and ❶ ______________. However, some of the vitamin ❷ ______________ may be lost when fruits and vegetables are ❸ ______________. Some fruits have a tough outer skin, but other fruit and vegetable skins can be eaten. Apple skin contains many vitamins as well as calcium and ❹ ______________. Potato skins have vitamin C and various minerals. Plant skins also contain fiber and ❺ ______________. Fiber can help people maintain a healthy weight. Antioxidants may help prevent ❻ ______________.

Unit 2 Deep Sleep and the Body

Vocabulary

A Match the words with their correct meanings.

tissue	linked to	achieve	exhausted	refreshed

1 feeling very tired ________________

2 to reach a goal ________________

3 muscle, organs, and skin ________________

4 feeling well-rested ________________

5 suggesting a relationship between two things ________________

B Choose the words from the box to complete the sentences.

exhausted	brain waves	cycle	strengthen

1 The machine measures ________________ during sleep.

2 Eating healthy foods can ________________ the immune system.

3 It is important to sleep well to avoid feeling ________________.

4 The sleep ________________ repeats several times in a single night.

Translation

C Read the sentences and translate them into your language.

1 People can sleep for nine hours but still feel exhausted.

➜ ____

2 The brain then moves into REM sleep, which speeds up body functions again.

➜ ____

3 Lack of deep sleep is linked to certain disorders and diseases.

➜ ____

Paraphrasing

D **Paraphrase the sentences from the passage with the words in the box.**

keeps	hard	revitalized	adequate
because	difficulty	assume	

1 It's generally believed that more sleep means a healthier mind and body.

→ People often ________________ sleeping more ________________ your mind and body healthy.

2 It's difficult to wake from this stage, as brain waves are very slow.

→ ________________ brain waves are so slow, it's ________________ to wake up from this stage.

3 People who undergo several cycles of deep sleep will wake up feeling rested and refreshed.

→ Those who undergo several deep sleep cycles will feel rested and ________________ when they wake.

4 Without enough deep sleep, people have trouble functioning.

→ People have ________________ functioning when they don't get ________________ deep sleep.

Listening

E **Listen to the summary and fill in the blanks.**

The ❶ ________________ of sleep is important for a healthy mind and body. There are two ❷ ________________ of sleep: REM and non-REM sleep. There are three stages of non-REM sleep, with deep sleep happening in stage 3. Deep sleep ❸ ________________ the most health benefits for the body and mind. During deep sleep, the brain repairs damaged ❹ ________________ and bone while strengthening the ❺ ________________ system. Without enough deep sleep, it is harder to ❻ ________________, and the risk of disease increases.

Unit 3 Petra

Vocabulary

A **Match the words with their correct meanings.**

tomb	nomadic	abandon	outsider	earthquake

1 a place bodies are put after death ____________

2 not living in one place for a long period of time ____________

3 someone not belonging to the group ____________

4 a natural event that shakes the ground ____________

5 to leave behind ____________

B **Choose the words from the box to complete the sentences.**

explorer	mosaic	harsh	nomadic

1 Most ancient people were ____________ and moved often.

2 They built stone homes to survive in the ____________ climate.

3 A colorful ____________ covered the walls of the old temple.

4 The ____________ discovered the lost city centuries later.

Translation

C **Read the sentences and translate them into your language.**

1 Known as the Rose City for its pinkish stone, the site is made up of caves, temples, and tombs.

➜ ____________

2 In addition, the strong cliffs made it difficult for outsiders to invade.

➜ ____________

3 The city has even been featured in popular films.

➜ ____________

Paraphrasing

D **Paraphrase the sentences from the passage with the words in the box.**

much	arrived	erected	offered
constructed	buildings	unforgiving	

1 However, not a lot is known about the people who built it.

→ But we do not know ________________ about the civilization that ________________ it.

2 These caves provided shelter from the harsh desert.

→ The caves ________________ protection from the ________________ desert.

3 Christianity came to Petra a few centuries later, and churches were built in the city.

→ A few centuries later, Christianity ________________ in Petra and churches were ________________ in the city.

4 Tourists also travel to Jordan to see the unique structures.

→ Additionally, tourists visit Jordan to view the unique ________________.

Listening

E **Listen to the summary and fill in the blanks.**

Petra, also called the Rose City, is an archaeological ❶ ________________ in modern-day Jordan. Thousands of years ago, the Nabateans began ❷ ________________ caves into cliffs. These caves provided shelter from the harsh desert. Petra became an important place for ❸ ________________ to stop in the desert. In 63 BC, the Romans arrived and built mosaics, ❹ ________________, and eventually churches. Petra was abandoned after an earthquake but was ❺ ________________ in 1812. Today, many of the buildings are still buried under sand. Tourists travel to the city to see the unique ❻ ________________.

Unit 4 Lucy

Vocabulary

A **Match the words with their correct meanings.**

evolution	map	ancestor	fossil	split

1 an early animal others have evolved from ______________

2 the remains of an ancient creature ______________

3 the slow development of something ______________

4 to divide into two or more groups ______________

5 to record in detail ______________

B **Choose the words from the box to complete the sentences.**

upright	fossils	valley	skeleton

1 The ancient tools were found in a ______________ in France.

2 Some human ancestors could not walk ______________.

3 The archaeologist dug up a dinosaur ______________.

4 When will the museum put the ______________ on display?

Translation

C **Read the sentences and translate them into your language.**

1 Johanson knew he had found something special.

→ ______________________________

2 Lucy is considered one of the most important fossils.

→ ______________________________

3 Decades later, scientists no longer believe Lucy is the key.

→ ______________________________

Paraphrasing

D **Paraphrase the sentences from the passage with the words in the box.**

might	holes	discovered	completely
prior to	initially	came from	

1 They all belonged to one amazing skeleton.

→ All of them ________________ one incredible skeleton.

2 At first, Johanson thought he had found a monkey.

→ ________________, Johanson believed he had ________________ a monkey.

3 Before Lucy was found, scientists did not fully understand human evolution.

→ ________________ finding Lucy, scientists did not ________________ grasp human evolution.

4 Lucy may have been a human ancestor, but there are still many gaps in the chain of human evolution.

→ Although Lucy ________________ have been a human ancestor, numerous ________________ remain in the chain of human evolution.

Listening

E **Listen to the summary and fill in the blanks.**

In 1974, Donald Johanson found a special ❶ ________________ in a valley in Ethiopia. This skeleton belonged to the Australopithecus ❷ ________________. This species lived around 3.7 million years ago and looked similar to apes. ❸ ________________ Lucy, the skeleton is a very important fossil. Scientists believed Lucy was the key to mapping ❹ ________________ evolution. Today, however, there are still many ❺ ________________ in the chain. Scientists continue to study Lucy and other fossils. They hope to map the ❻ ________________ of evolution.

Unit 5 The Age of the Sun

Vocabulary

A **Match the words with their correct meanings.**

expel	expand	transition	task	sustain

1 a change from one state to another ______________

2 to keep alive ______________

3 a job that is done ______________

4 to release ______________

5 to grow larger ______________

B **Choose the words from the box to complete the sentences.**

sustain	dense	vaporize	predict

1 Scientists ______________ the sun will become a nebula.

2 The heat caused the planet's oceans to ______________.

3 The moon is made up of ______________ rocky material.

4 What conditions are needed to ______________ life?

Translation

C **Read the sentences and translate them into your language.**

1 Dwarf stars are small but hot and bright enough to sustain life from a distance.

→ ______________________________

2 Determining the sun's age was no easy task.

→ ______________________________

3 The sun will become so large that it will consume the first three planets.

→ ______________________________

Paraphrasing

D Paraphrase the sentences from the passage with the words in the box.

midpoint	release	increase	formed
generate	examine	guess	

1 Solar astronomers estimate that the sun is somewhere in the middle of its life cycle.

→ Solar astronomers ________________ that the sun is approximately at the ________________ of its life cycle.

2 Since the planets came together around the same time, it was useful to study the entire solar system.

→ Because the planets ________________ around the same time, it was helpful to ________________ the whole solar system.

3 Red giants are much larger than dwarf stars, which means the sun will expand outward.

→ Red giants are a lot bigger than dwarf stars, so the sun will ________________ in diameter.

4 The white dwarf will produce its last light and then expel its remaining gases.

→ The white dwarf will ________________ its final light and then ________________ its leftover gases.

Listening

E Listen to the summary and fill in the blanks.

Earth's sun is around 4.6 billion years old and is in the middle of its ❶ ________________. Determining the sun's age was difficult, but ❷ ________________ helped with this. The sun will later grow into a red giant and ❸ ________________ the first three planets. Earth's ❹ ________________ will vaporize, and the planet will no longer sustain life. Then the sun will begin to die and become a white dwarf, a ❺ ________________ type of star. The white dwarf will expel its gases and become a ❻ ________________ nebula.

Unit 6 Comets vs. Asteroids

Vocabulary

A Match the words with their correct meanings.

orbit	form	composition	vary	body

1 an object in space ____________

2 to move in a fixed path around an object ____________

3 to combine to create something ____________

4 what a substance is made of ____________

5 to differ in size or quality ____________

B Choose the words from the box to complete the sentences.

telescopes	vary	tail	composition

1 Today, high-tech ____________ are used to look at stars.

2 It was difficult to determine the meteor's ____________.

3 Asteroids and comets ____________ greatly in size and shape.

4 A ____________ of light followed the meteor as it fell from the sky.

Translation

C Read the sentences and translate them into your language.

1 Comets and asteroids are small bodies of matter that travel through space.

➜ ____________

2 The solar system's comets and asteroids formed around the same time as the planets.

➜ ____________

3 When a comet is far from the sun, it remains frozen.

➜ ____________

Paraphrasing

D **Paraphrase the sentences from the passage with the words in the box.**

revolve around	categorized	alternatively	fairly
composed	travel	distance	

1 These bodies orbit the sun in unique paths.

→ These bodies ________________ the sun in unique routes.

2 Asteroids formed quite close to the sun while comets formed much farther away.

→ Asteroids formed ________________ close to the sun, but comets formed at a much greater ________________.

3 They are not large enough to be considered planets, but they orbit the sun just like planets do.

→ They are too small to be ________________ as planets, but they ________________ around the sun just as planets do.

4 Comets, on the other hand, are made up of ice, gases, and rock.

→ ________________, comets are ________________ of ice, gases, and rock.

Listening

E **Listen to the summary and fill in the blanks.**

❶ ________________ and asteroids are small bodies of matter that ❷ ________________ through space. Most comets and asteroids are thought to be around 4.5 billion years old. However, they have some key differences. ❸ ________________ are mostly made up of metals and rock. They formed close to the sun, so they don't have any ❹ ________________. Comets, on the other hand, have ❺ ________________ orbits. Sometimes, they pass close to the sun before traveling farther away. When a comet passes close to the sun, some of the ice and gases ❻ ________________, creating tails of dust.

Unit 7 Armored Animals

Vocabulary

A **Match the words with their correct meanings.**

sting	pincer	defend	wound	shield

1 to pierce the skin with a stinger ____________

2 an object used to protect against harm ____________

3 to hurt a living creature ____________

4 the claw of a crab or lobster ____________

5 to protect against an attack ____________

B **Choose the words from the box to complete the sentences.**

sensed	tuck	camouflage	pincer

1 Many reptiles use ____________ to hide from predators.

2 The rabbit ____________ danger and quickly ran away.

3 The crab used its ____________ to catch some food.

4 When frightened, turtles ____________ their legs inside.

Translation

C **Read the sentences and translate them into your language.**

1 Certain animals use camouflage to blend in with their surroundings.

→ ____________

2 Predators have a difficult time wounding an armadillo.

→ ____________

3 Turtles and tortoises both have hard shells that are made up of bones covered by plates.

→ ____________

Paraphrasing

D **Paraphrase the sentences from the passage with the words in the box.**

assist	limbs	violent	discharging
stab	upright	threatened	

1 Others are more aggressive and may bite or sting, releasing deadly poisons.

→ Others are more ________________ and might bite or sting, ________________ lethal toxins.

2 Their quills stand erect, ready to pierce approaching predators.

→ Their quills stand ________________, prepared to ________________ nearing predators.

3 When there is danger, these animals will draw their legs and feet inside the shell.

→ When ________________, these creatures will pull their ________________ into their shells.

4 They also have pincers to help defend against predators.

→ They also have pincers to ________________ in guarding against predators.

Listening

E **Listen to the summary and fill in the blanks.**

Animals have different types of ❶ ________________ to protect themselves from predators. Armadillos have bony ❷ ________________ while porcupines are covered in sharp ❸ ________________. Predators have a hard time eating these animals. Likewise, turtles and tortoises both have hard shells. They draw their legs in and tuck their heads inside. ❹ ________________ are unable to bite through their hard shells. Certain land and sea animals have ❺ ________________ covering their soft insides. All of these animals use their armor to ❻ ________________ themselves against danger.

Unit 8 Social vs. Solitary Animals

Vocabulary

A **Match the words with their correct meanings.**

complex	offspring	obey	savannah	male

1 a flat grassy area ____________
2 a boy or a man ____________
3 to follow rules or requests ____________
4 not simple ____________
5 the babies of a particular animal ____________

B **Choose the words from the box to complete the sentences.**

offspring	due to	stalked	pack

1 A ____________ of wolves was seen hunting in the forest.
2 ____________ the cold, foxes need thick coats of fur.
3 Female cats can give birth to numerous ____________.
4 The lion quietly ____________ its prey before pouncing.

Translation

C **Read the sentences and translate them into your language.**

1 A lion pride works together to hunt, defend their territory, and care for their young.
→ ____________

2 One male and one female are considered the leaders of the pack.
→ ____________

3 Living in a large herd keeps elephants safe from predators.
→ ____________

Paraphrasing

D **Paraphrase the sentences from the passage with the words in the box.**

wilderness	as soon as	team	track
by themselves	go back	intricate	

1 Alone, they may have trouble surviving in the wild.

→ ________________, they could have difficulty staying alive in the ________________.

2 When they hunt, they work together to stalk and kill large animals.

→ While hunting, they work as a ________________ to ________________ and kill big animals.

3 They form complex relationships with each other.

→ They develop ________________ relationships with each other.

4 Once mating season is over, they return to their solitary lives.

→ ________________ mating season is finished, they ________________ to their solitary lives.

Listening

E **Listen to the summary and fill in the blanks.**

When we think of animals living in groups, we often imagine a ❶ ________________ of lions. However, many other animals also live in groups. ❷ ________________ live in packs that have a social hierarchy. One male and one female are considered the ❸ ________________ of the pack. Non-predatory animals, like elephants, also live in groups. An elephant herd follows the ❹ ________________ female. On the other hand, some animals prefer to live ❺ ________________. Tigers are extremely territorial and do not like to share ❻ ________________.

Unit 9 Famous Pirates

Vocabulary

A **Match the words with their correct meanings.**

execution	take over	capture	merchant	brutal

1 harsh or violent ______________

2 to catch ______________

3 a person or company that arranges trade or supplies goods ______________

4 when the state puts a criminal to death ______________

5 to assume control of ______________

B **Choose the words from the box to complete the sentences.**

portrayal	fierce	riches	capture

1 The film's ______________ of the king was incorrect.

2 The ship captain was known to be very ______________.

3 How did the soldiers ______________ the prisoner?

4 The tomb was filled with the queen's ______________.

Translation

C **Read the sentences and translate them into your language.**

1 Many fictional pirate characters are based on real pirates.

➜ ______________________________

2 Better known by his nickname, Blackbeard, he was born in England in 1680.

➜ ______________________________

3 Bonny joined Rackham's crew while dressing and behaving like a man.

➜ ______________________________

Paraphrasing

D **Paraphrase the sentences from the passage with the words in the box.**

prosperous	agreement	ruthless	ultimately
generated	presented	depictions	

1 Production companies like Disney have made millions of dollars for their portrayals of pirates.

→ Film companies, such as Disney, have ________________ millions of dollars for their ________________ of pirates.

2 He wasn't the most successful pirate, but he is remembered as being one of the most brutal.

→ Although he wasn't the most ________________ pirate, he is known as being one of the most ________________.

3 However, Bonny was eventually captured along with Rackham's crew.

→ Nevertheless, Bonny was ________________ caught with Rackham's crew.

4 Ching Shih became so powerful that the Chinese government offered her a peace deal.

→ As a result of Ching Shih's power, the Chinese government ________________ her with a peace ________________.

Listening

E **Listen to the summary and fill in the blanks.**

Pirates are popular TV and film characters, but many are based on real pirates. Edward Teach, better known as Blackbeard, wasn't the most ❶ ________________ pirate. However, he was one of the most ❷ ________________. Anne Bonny and "Calico" Jack Rackham were the most famous pirate couple. Together, they were a ❸ ________________ team, but Bonny was eventually captured. No one knows what ❹ ________________ to her. The most successful ❺ ________________ pirate was Ching Shih. She commanded over 1,500 ships and 80,000 men. This is more than all the well-known pirates ❻ ________________.

Unit 10 Spartan Society

Vocabulary

A **Match the words with their correct meanings.**

position of power	slave	rigid	founder	generation

1 strict; not flexible ____________

2 a group of people born within a few years ____________

3 a person who starts an organization or town ____________

4 a ruling position, such as a king or president ____________

5 a person forced to work without pay or freedom ____________

B **Choose the words from the box to complete the sentences.**

conducted	invaded	warrior	founder

1 The ____________ carried a sword and a heavy shield.

2 A massive statue was erected for the city's ____________.

3 The Romans commonly ____________ nearby regions.

4 They ____________ all their business in the city square.

Translation

C **Read the sentences and translate them into your language.**

1 Ancient Greece was made up of many cultures.

➜ ____

2 This made them valuable to the Spartiate class.

➜ ____

3 Helots could win their freedom by serving in the military.

➜ ____

Paraphrasing

D **Paraphrase the sentences from the passage with the words in the box.**

authority	lineage	enslaved	permitted
all else	map	allegiance	

1 Spartans valued loyalty and military service more than anything.

→ Spartans prized ______________ and military service above ______________.

2 Usually, they could trace their ancestry back to the founders of the city.

→ Typically, they could ______________ their ______________ back to the founders of the city.

3 They were not allowed to have positions of power.

→ They were not ______________ to occupy positions of ______________.

4 Spartans killed many helots and took others as slaves.

→ Many helots were killed by Spartans and others were ______________.

Listening

E **Listen to the summary and fill in the blanks.**

Ancient Sparta had a very ❶ ______________ class structure with three main classes. The Spartiate had lived in Sparta for many generations. They were ❷ ______________ and made all important decisions for Sparta. The perioeci were a ❸ ______________ below the Spartiate but had many rights. They could own land, serve in the ❹ ______________, and conduct trade. At the bottom were the helots, who were hated by most Spartans. Helots could win their ❺ ______________ by serving in the military, but they were still ❻ ______________ poorly.

Unit 11 Mirages

Vocabulary

A **Match the words with their correct meanings.**

surface	illusion	disappear	spectacular	bend

1 to not be visible anymore ____________

2 a thing that confuses the senses ____________

3 a curve; to shape something into a curve ____________

4 the top layer of something ____________

5 beautiful in a dramatic way ____________

B **Choose the words from the box to complete the sentences.**

register	temperature	surface	glittered

1 The ocean ____________ in the afternoon sunlight.

2 The ____________ dropped steadily in winter.

3 He could not ____________ the change in the wind.

4 A thin layer of ice covered the pond's ____________.

Translation

C **Read the sentences and translate them into your language.**

1 What you saw was only a mirage.

→ ____________

2 In deserts, the ground is often hotter than the air, which causes the air just above it to warm.

→ ____________

3 In the desert, this object appears to be the surface of water.

→ ____________

Paraphrasing

D **Paraphrase the sentences from the passage with the words in the box.**

fluctuates	cooler	sparkling	travels
unexpectedly	detect	areas	

1 Suddenly, you spot a glittering patch of water in the distance.

→ ________________, you see a ________________ patch of water in the distance.

2 Normally, light moves in a straight line, but the speed varies depending on the temperature of the air.

→ Usually, light ________________ in a straight path, but the speed ________________ based on the temperature of the air.

3 This illusion occurs because the human brain cannot register a bend in light.

→ This illusion happens because the human brain cannot ________________ a curve in light.

4 In some regions, the temperature close to the ground is colder than the air above it.

→ In certain ________________, the temperature near the surface is ________________ than the air over it.

Listening

E **Listen to the summary and fill in the blanks.**

Mirages occur when the air close to the ground is ❶ ________________ than the air above it. When light hits this warmer air, it ❷ ________________ into a U-shape. This creates a ❸ ________________ effect, like sunlight shining across water. The human brain can't ❹ ________________ a bend in light, so we assume it's an object. This can also occur when temperatures are reversed. Light bends up and ❺ ________________ an image above a real object. These mirages are common in colder ❻ ________________ and near oceans.

Unit 12 Fire Behavior and Weather

Vocabulary

A Match the words with their correct meanings.

abruptly	steadily	factor	supply	fuel

1 a circumstance or condition ____________
2 something that can burn easily ____________
3 without stopping ____________
4 the amount of resources ____________
5 quickly; without notice ____________

B Choose the words from the box to complete the sentences.

steadily	mild	moisture	enormous

1 The forest fire burned ____________ for eight days.
2 An ____________ tornado formed over the field.
3 The humid summer air was full of ____________.
4 They expected the snow storm to be ____________.

Translation

C Read the sentences and translate them into your language.

1 When forest fires rage out of control, they can pose a threat to animal and human life.
→ ____________

2 The temperature of the fuels also determines how fast a fire will spread.
→ ____________

3 Blowing wind can increase a fire's oxygen supply, which causes the fire to grow larger.
→ ____________

Paraphrasing

D **Paraphrase the sentences from the passage with the words in the box.**

greatly	non-serious	subsequently	returns
areas	transferring	ignite	

1 In mild cases, fire burns away dying leaves and restores the health of the forest.

→ In ________________ instances, fire burns dying leaves and ________________ the forest to a healthy state.

2 This in turn heats forest fuels and can cause them to catch fire.

→ This ________________ warms forest fuels and can make them ________________.

3 Wind also fans the fire, essentially moving the flames to other parts of a forest or city.

→ In addition, wind fans the blaze, in essence ________________ the flames to other ________________ of a forest or city.

4 When the air's moisture content is low, the risk of a fire starting increases dramatically.

→ When the humidity is low, the chance of a fire igniting increases ________________.

Listening

E **Listen to the summary and fill in the blanks.**

Certain weather conditions can ❶ ________________ to the spread of forest fires. ❷ ________________ is one factor that can affect this spread. Light from the sun warms forest ❸ ________________. Warmer fuels will burn more ❹ ________________. This is why fires tend to burn hotter and spread faster in the middle of the day. Wind can also affect a fire's spread by increasing its oxygen ❺ ________________. Wind also fans the flames and can make a fire become unpredictable. Humidity is one of the most important factors in fire ❻ ________________. This means drier fuels tend to burn hotter and faster.

Unit 13 Evolving Gut Bacteria

Vocabulary

A Match the words with their correct meanings.

healthy	treat	gut	ethnic group	genetics

1 not sick or injured ________________

2 a group that shares a common cultural background ________________

3 the features of an organism, often found in DNA ________________

4 to provide medical care ________________

5 the lower part of the intestines ________________

B Choose the words from the box to complete the sentences.

for instance	treat	digest	evolve

1 Living creatures ________________ over thousands of years.

2 Are humans able to ________________ all types of plants?

3 The researcher found a new way to ________________ the disease.

4 Viruses, ________________, can be quite deadly to humans.

Translation

C Read the sentences and translate them into your language.

1 Firstly, a person's diet can affect gut bacteria.

→ ____

2 A person's immune system might also cause gut bacteria to change.

→ ____

3 Gender, age, and weight seem to have no effect on these bacteria.

→ ____

Paraphrasing

D **Paraphrase the sentences from the passage with the words in the box.**

someday	initially	processing	death
dreaded	cure	rapidly	

1 Bacteria species are often feared, as they can cause many terrible diseases.

→ Bacteria species are usually ________________, since they can cause many horrible infections.

2 At first, their gut bacteria will have a hard time digesting the fiber.

→ ________________, their gut bacteria will have trouble ________________ the fiber.

3 Scientists think gut bacteria change quickly to avoid being killed.

→ Scientists believe gut bacteria evolve ________________ to evade ________________.

4 In the future, gut bacteria could be used to treat illnesses.

→ ________________, gut bacteria might be used to ________________ diseases.

Listening

E **Listen to the summary and fill in the blanks.**

Since they can cause terrible ❶ ________________, bacteria are often feared. However, there are many ❷ ________________ bacteria species, such as gut bacteria. Gut bacteria can ❸ ________________ quickly to suit a person's body. Over time, gut bacteria will adapt to changes in a person's ❹ ________________. For example, they might adapt to a new type of fiber. Gut ❺ ________________ will also change in order to hide from the immune system. In the future, gut bacteria could be used to treat illnesses and ❻ ________________ problems.

Unit 14 Deep Sea Life

Vocabulary

A Match the words with their correct meanings.

lure	withstand	sense	segment	extreme

1 reaching a high degree ____________

2 one part of many ____________

3 to remain unaffected by a force ____________

4 a way something is observed; sight, sound, taste, touch, smell ____________

5 something that is used to attract an animal ____________

B Choose the words from the box to complete the sentences.

depths	sense	jaws	pressure

1 The ____________ increased as they swam deeper.

2 The mouse could ____________ the owl watching above.

3 Rare jellyfish can live at ____________ of 9,000 meters.

4 Sharks have strong ____________ filled with rows of teeth.

Translation

C Read the sentences and translate them into your language.

1 The lower the depth, the harsher the environment.

→ ____________

2 Its body has seven segments with numerous legs for walking and swimming.

→ ____________

3 This lure is attached to its head and is filled with light-producing bacteria.

→ ____________

Paraphrasing

D **Paraphrase the sentences from the passage with the words in the box.**

absence	environments	endure	exceptional
tough	increased	not much	

1 Some unique creatures can survive in these conditions.

→ Some special animals can live in these ________________.

2 The giant isopod has adapted to withstand the cold temperature and high pressure.

→ The giant isopod has evolved to ________________ the low temperature and ________________ pressure.

3 Since little sunlight reaches the deep sea, this predator needs to have excellent senses.

→ As ________________ sunlight enters the deep sea, this hunter requires ________________ senses.

4 Sunlight is completely absent there, which makes it difficult for fish to attract prey.

→ The ________________ of sunlight there makes it ________________ for fish to bait prey.

Listening

E **Listen to the summary and fill in the blanks.**

The oceans are harsh environments, but some ❶ ________________ can survive in extreme conditions. The giant isopod can be found 2,400 meters below the ❷ ________________. There, it feeds on dead sea creatures, such as whales, fish, and squid. The hammerhead ❸ ________________ swims in depths of 600 meters. Its hammer-shaped ❹ ________________ helps it see prey better. It must also have excellent senses. The anglerfish lives at ❺ ________________ of at least 2,000 meters. Sunlight is absent, so the anglerfish uses a lure to ❻ ________________ its prey.

Unit 15 Ventriloquism

Vocabulary

A Match the words with their correct meanings.

competition	renew	carnival	witchcraft	oracle

1 someone who tells the future ____________

2 magic done by a witch ____________

3 a traveling festival ____________

4 a contest of skill ____________

5 to begin again; to make new again ____________

B Choose the words from the box to complete the sentences.

prediction	renew	interest	religious

1 ____________ practices tend to vary from region to region.

2 The carnival fortune teller made a scary ____________.

3 The exhibit generated a lot of ____________ in modern art.

4 Did you ____________ your theater membership last month?

Translation

C Read the sentences and translate them into your language.

1 Modern ventriloquists are known as stage performers.

→ ____

2 It was no longer seen as a religious practice.

→ ____

3 It sounded as though his voice was coming from somewhere else.

→ ____

Paraphrasing

D Paraphrase the sentences from the passage with the words in the box.

sounds	notice	developed	reestablished
as a result	deemed	prophets	

1 Oracles listened to the noises and made predictions.

→ ________________ heard the ________________ and predicted the future.

2 Thus, anyone who performed was considered a witch.

→ ________________, those who performed were ________________ witches.

3 A ventriloquist created a special voice for each of his dummies.

→ A ventriloquist ________________ a unique voice for all of his dolls.

4 This renewed the public's interest in ventriloquism.

→ This ________________ the people's ________________ of ventriloquism.

Listening

E Listen to the summary and fill in the blanks.

Modern ventriloquism is a stage performance, but it wasn't always this way. In ancient Greece, ventriloquism was a religious practice done by ❶ ________________. They believed the dead lived inside the human stomach. Oracles listened to sounds made by the stomach and made ❷ ________________. By the Middle Ages, ventriloquism was considered a form of ❸ ________________. In the 1800s, ventriloquists traveled with ❹ ________________ and performed on stages. They began using ❺ ________________ during performances. Ventriloquism lost popularity in the 20th century, but talent competitions ❻ ________________ the public's interest.

Unit 16 African Cave Art

Vocabulary

A Match the words with their correct meanings.

recent	prize	continent	pattern	migrate

1. to value highly ______________
2. a design of repeating lines or shapes ______________
3. close to the present ______________
4. a landmass often containing more than one country ______________
5. to move from one area to another, often seasonal ______________

B Choose the words from the box to complete the sentences.

well-preserved	continents	herders	date back to

1. The performers traveled across three ______________.
2. The *Mona Lisa* is a ______________ Da Vinci painting.
3. These manuscripts ______________ the 15th century CE.
4. All of the artwork depicted ______________ guiding cattle.

Translation

C Read the sentences and translate them into your language.

1. The lives of hunter-gatherers were focused mainly on animals.

   → ______________________________

2. Africa is rich with more recent cave art as well.

   → ______________________________

3. The most well-preserved cave art can be found in North Africa.

   → ______________________________

Paraphrasing

D **Paraphrase the sentences from the passage with the words in the box.**

depict	discovered	valued	approximately
houses	civilizations	in addition to	

1 Like all societies, early humans prized art.

→ As with all ______________, ancient humans ______________ art.

2 The Apollo 11 cave contains some of the oldest art ever found.

→ The Apollo 11 cave ______________ some of the most ancient art ever ______________.

3 These paintings may have been created around 5,000 years ago.

→ These images might have been painted ______________ 5,000 years ago.

4 These paintings show migrating animals as well as changes in the weather.

→ These paintings ______________ migrating animals ______________ fluctuations in the weather.

Listening

E **Listen to the summary and fill in the blanks.**

Many early humans painted on the walls of ❶ ______________. Africa boasts some of the most well-preserved cave art on the planet. The Apollo 11 cave, located in Namibia, contains some of the ❷ ______________ art ever found. However, the oldest rock ❸ ______________ was discovered in South Africa. Africa is also rich with more recent art. ❹ ______________ have discovered numerous paintings of animals, herders, and hunters on horseback. The most ❺ ______________ cave art can be found in North Africa. Caves in Algeria and Egypt contain ❻ ______________ of incredible images.

Further Writing Practice

Unit 1 Healthy Plant Skins

Q **Choose a fruit or vegetable you like and write about it. Describe its vitamin content and uses.**

A The following table shows some ideas for answering the question above. Check the one that you like the most. If you have your own idea, write it in the last row.

Fruit or Vegetable	Vitamin Content and Uses
☐ Banana / Fruit	• contains high levels of vitamins B6, B12, and potassium • eat it raw, bake it in muffins, or make a fruit salad
☐ Zucchini / Vegetable	• has vitamins B6, C, and K, as well as many minerals • grill it or add it to delicious pastas and soups
☐ Carrot / Vegetable	• is a good source of vitamins A, K, and B6 • put it in salads and soups or make carrot cake

B Read the question again and complete the following paragraph.

A(n) ______________________ is a ______________________ I like to eat.
It ____.
I can ____
____.

Unit 2 Deep Sleep and the Body

Q **What helps you fall asleep easily? Choose a method and write about it.**

A The following table shows some ideas for answering the question above. Check the one that you like the most. If you have your own idea, write it in the last row.

Method	Description and Effect
☐ Reading Books	• lay in bed and read a relaxing storybook • helps my body and mind relax so I can fall asleep
☐ Meditating	• go to a quiet place and clear the thoughts from my mind • helps me relieve stress so I don't focus on my worries
☐ Doing Yoga	• sit on my yoga mat and do a variety of stretches • lowers my heart rate and calms me down before bed

B Read the question again and complete the following paragraph.

________________________________ is a great way to fall asleep easily.

Before I go to sleep, I ________________________________

________________________________. This ________________________________

________________________________.

Unit 3 Petra

Q **Choose an interesting ancient place. What is it and who built it?**

A The following table shows some ideas for answering the question above. Check the one that you like the most. If you have your own idea, write it in the last row.

Place	Type and Founders
☐ Angkor Wat	• an ancient temple found in modern-day Cambodia • by the Khmer Empire in the 12th century
☐ Machu Picchu	• an ancient ruin located in Peru, South America • by the ninth ruler of the Inca sometime in the 1400s
☐ The Great Pyramid	• the largest pyramid on the Giza Plateau in Egypt • as a tomb for the Egyptian pharaoh Khufu

B Read the question again and complete the following paragraph.

____________________ is an interesting ancient place. It is ____________________ ____________________. It was built ____________________ ____________________.

Unit 4 Lucy

Q Choose an important artifact or site and write about it. How was it discovered?

A The following table shows some ideas for answering the question above. Check the one that you like the most. If you have your own idea, write it in the last row.

Site	Description and Discovery
☐ Qin Shi Huang's Terracotta Army	• a collection of statues that were buried underground • discovered by a farmer who was drilling for water in 1947
☐ The Dead Sea Scrolls	• a collection of ancient manuscripts, mostly biblical • found at several sites on the shore of the Dead Sea
☐ The Rosetta Stone	• a stone slab that has inscriptions in three languages • discovered in 1799 by a French soldier in Egypt

B Read the question again and complete the following paragraph.

________________________________ is/are (an) important artifact(s).

It is/They are ________________________________

________________________________. It was/They were ________________________________

________________________________.

Unit 5 The Age of the Sun

Q Choose a type of star you find interesting and write about it.

A The following table shows some ideas for answering the question above. Check the one that you like the most. If you have your own idea, write it in the last row.

Type	Size and Brightness
☐ Red Giant	• average in size, around 30 times the size of our sun • are bright but cool and appear red or orange in color
☐ Blue Giant	• about ten times the mass of Earth's sun • are the hottest and brightest stars in the universe
☐ Supergiant	• the biggest, often hundreds of millions of miles wide • come in a range of temperatures and brightness

B Read the question again and complete the following paragraph.

A ______________________ is a type of star I find interesting.
This type of star is ______________________
______________________. These stars ______________________
______________________.

Unit 6 Comets vs. Asteroids

Q **Write about a celestial body in our solar system. What is it made of?**

A The following table shows some ideas for answering the question above. Check the one that you like the most. If you have your own idea, write it in the last row.

Object	Type and Composition
☐ Jupiter	• the largest gas giant orbiting the sun in our solar system • gases, mainly hydrogen and helium, and other elements
☐ Pluto	• a dwarf planet located at the edge of our solar system • a mixture of 70 percent rock and 30 percent ice
☐ Halley's Comet	• a comet that can be seen from Earth every 75-76 years • a combination of ice, gases, and dust

B Read the question again and complete the following paragraph.

____________________ is a celestial body in our solar system. It is ____________________ ____________________. It is made up of ____________________ ____________________.

Unit 7 Armored Animals

Q **Write about an animal that uses camouflage. What features help it hide?**

A The following table shows some ideas for answering the question above. Check the one that you like the most. If you have your own idea, write it in the last row.

Animal	Where it Lives and How it Hides
☐ Polar Bear	• in the ice and snow of the Arctic and northern Canada • it uses its white fur to blend in with the ice
☐ Chameleon	• primarily in Africa but can be found on other continents • it changes its body color to match its surroundings
☐ Leafy Seadragon	• along the southern and western coasts of Australia • it waves its leaf-shaped body so it looks like a plant

B Read the question again and complete the following paragraph.

A ______________________ is an animal that uses camouflage. It lives ______________________ ______________________. To hide from predators, ______________________ ______________________.

Unit 8 Social vs. Solitary Animals

Q **Write about an interesting solitary animal. When does it become social?**

A The following table shows some ideas for answering the question above. Check the one that you like the most. If you have your own idea, write it in the last row.

Animal	Where They Live and Exceptions
☐ Platypuses	• spend their lives alone in rivers and on riverbanks • their territories overlap with other platypuses
☐ Skunks	• prefer to live and look for food alone in forests • they share dens with other skunks in winter to stay warm
☐ Koalas	• would rather climb trees alone in Australian forests • they meet other koalas during mating season

B Read the question again and complete the following paragraph.

____________________________ are interesting solitary animals. These animals ____________________________ ____________________. However, sometimes ____________________ ____________________________________.

Unit 9 Famous Pirates

Q **Write about a famous criminal in history.**

A The following table shows some ideas for answering the question above. Check the one that you like the most. If you have your own idea, write it in the last row.

Name	Life and Death
☐ Billy the Kid	• a famous American gunfighter in the Old West • was killed at the age of 21 by a local sheriff
☐ Sir Henry Morgan	• a pirate who pillaged the Caribbean in the 1600s • moved to Jamaica during a war between England and Spain
☐ Jesse James	• an American outlaw who robbed banks and trains • was shot in the back and killed by a fellow gang member

B Read the question again and complete the following paragraph.

____________________________ was a well-known criminal.
He/She was ____________________________________
____________________. Eventually, he/she ________________
____.

Unit 10 Spartan Society

Q **Write about an ancient city you want to see. What happened to it?**

A The following table shows some ideas for answering the question above. Check the one that you like the most. If you have your own idea, write it in the last row.

City	Location and Decline
☐ Thonis	• an ancient city in Egypt called "The Gateway to Egypt" • was drowned by the Mediterranean Sea in the 8th century
☐ Pompeii	• a Roman city founded in the 6th or 7th century BCE • was destroyed when Mount Vesuvius erupted
☐ Palenque	• a Mayan city that was inhabited from 700-1100 CE • declined as a result of warfare, famine, and climate change

B Read the question again and complete the following paragraph.

I want to see the ancient city of ______________________.
It was ____
______________________. In the end, it ______________________
____.

Unit 11 Mirages

Q **Write about a weather phenomenon you have seen. What causes it?**

A The following table shows some ideas for answering the question above. Check the one that you like the most. If you have your own idea, write it in the last row.

Phenomenon	Appearance and Cause
☐ Fog	• the clouds have fallen and covered the ground • water vapor turns into small water droplets in the air
☐ A Dust Storm	• sheets of sand moving across the desert • heavy winds sweep up loose sand and dirt
☐ Hail	• balls of ice falling from the sky during a storm • wind sweeps water high up where it freezes into lumps

B Read the question again and complete the following paragraph.

____________________ is a weather phenomenon I have seen.
It looks like ______________________________
____________________. It occurs when ____________________
____.

Unit 12 Fire Behavior and Weather

Q **Why are forests important? Give an example.**

A The following table shows some ideas for answering the question above. Check the one that you like the most. If you have your own idea, write it in the last row.

Reason	Example and Possible Dangers
☐ Provide Oxygen	• clean the air and produce the oxygen we need to breathe • greenhouse gases will cause climate change to accelerate
☐ Shelter Animals	• provide shelter for numerous animal species • many species will go extinct when they lose their homes
☐ Prevent Disasters	• offer safety to humans and animals alike • floods, landslides, and dust storms will occur more often

B Read the question again and complete the following paragraph.

Forests are important because they ______________________________.
For example, trees ______________________________
______________________________. Without forests, ______________________________
______________________________.

Unit 13 Evolving Gut Bacteria

Q **How can you maintain healthy gut bacteria?**

A The following table shows some ideas for answering the question above. Check the one that you like the most. If you have your own idea, write it in the last row.

Method	Reason and Effect
☐ Eating Yogurt	• yogurt contains probiotics, or healthy gut bacteria • eating yogurt will improve your overall digestion
☐ Exercising	• exercise can get your digestive system moving • exercising boosts metabolism and reduces stomachaches
☐ Avoiding Sweeteners	• artificial sweeteners can increase harmful bacteria • avoiding sweeteners can prevent certain diseases

B Read the question again and complete the following paragraph.

____________________ is one way to maintain healthy gut bacteria. This is effective because ____________________ ____________________. Therefore, ____________________ ____________________.

Unit 14 Deep Sea Life

Q **Describe a way deep-sea creatures catch prey. Name an animal that uses this method.**

A The following table shows some ideas for answering the question above. Check the one that you like the most. If you have your own idea, write it in the last row.

Method	Description and Example
☐ A Lure	• a light or tentacle that fools and attracts prey • the deep-sea squid uses a long tentacle to fool fish
☐ Using Senses	• the ability to smell or feel when prey is nearby • sharks can smell blood as well as detect vibrations
☐ Speed	• the ability to move quickly by swimming or walking • the Japanese spider crab uses its long legs to stalk prey

B Read the question again and complete the following paragraph.

____________________ is one way certain deep-sea creatures hunt. It is ____. For example, ____.

Unit 15 Ventriloquism

Q What stage performance would you like to watch?

A The following table shows some ideas for answering the question above. Check the one that you like the most. If you have your own idea, write it in the last row.

Performance	Description and Reason
☐ Musical	• like a stage play but with a lot of singing and dancing • I enjoy music, and I want to be an actor when I grow up
☐ Stand-Up Comedy	• a comedy performance done by a single comedian • I think comedians are very smart, and I enjoy jokes
☐ Ballet	• a classical dance performance done by skilled dancers • the dances are so beautiful, and the dancers are talented

B Read the question again and complete the following paragraph.

I would like to watch a(n) ______________________________ performance.
It is ____
______________________. I want to watch this performance because ____________
____.

Unit 16 African Cave Art

Q **What famous art would you like to see and why?**

A The following table shows some ideas for answering the question above. Check the one that you like the most. If you have your own idea, write it in the last row.

Artwork	Location and Reason
☐ *The Scream*	• an Edvard Munch painting in the National Gallery in Norway • I think the painting is mysterious and full of emotion
☐ The Sistine Ceiling	• a painted ceiling in the Sistine Chapel in Rome • I am a fan of Michelangelo's incredible artworks
☐ Lascaux	• a complex of caves located in southwestern France • I want to see the various ancient wall paintings there

B Read the question again and complete the following paragraph.

Of all the famous artworks, I would most like to see ______________________. It is ____ ______________________. I want to see it because ______________________ ____.

MEMO

Fundamental
Reading
BASIC 2